A PORTION OF MY SPIRIT

A PORTION OF MY SPIRIT

THE CATHOLIC CHARISMATIC RENEWAL

BY
MICHAEL SCANLAN, T.O.R.

CARILLON BOOKS

ST. PAUL, MINNESOTA

First published 1979

A PORTION OF MY SPIRIT:
The Catholic Charismatic Renewal

A Carillon Book

Carillon Books Edition published 1979

ISBN: 0-89310-047-1   (Hardcover)
        0-89310-048-X   (Paperback)

Library of Congress Catalog Card Number 79-51723

Carillon Books
2115 Summit Avenue
St. Paul, Minnesota 55105 U.S.A.

Nothing Contrary to Faith:
   Rev. Christian Oravec, T.O.R., S.T.D.
   Rev. Daniel Sinisi, T.O.R., M.A., S.T.L.

Approved:
   Very Rev. Edmund Carroll, T.O.R.
   Minister Provincial

All Scripture quotations are from the Revised Standard
Version and the New American Bible.

Printed in the United States of America

TABLE OF CONTENTS

FOREWORD

I welcome the opportunity to write for you. I am a Franciscan priest who has held many leadership positions in the Catholic Charismatic Renewal, and who has participated in the major events of the renewal over the past nine years. In 1977 I was chairman of the National Service Committee of the Catholic Charismatic Renewal which takes a pastoral concern for the renewal in the United States. I am a former rector of a major seminary as well as a former practicing attorney. I presently serve as President of the College of Steubenville, Steubenville, Ohio.

This book is ambitious in subject matter. Frankly it would be too ambitious if it intended to give a comprehensive picture of the charismatic renewal. What I have done instead is to give a perspective on the renewal which will enable all Catholics to understand where it came from, what's going on in it and where it's headed. This book is written in order to achieve these results for you.

I have therefore woven together factual information and theological reflections with a personal perspective. The prominent psychologist, Dr. Carl Rogers, achieved a

new insight into the means of gaining rapport in coun-
selling with his teaching on the importance of being
deeply personal in building a relationship. He coined
the phrase, "What is most personal is most universal."
People identify more easily with us the more we reveal
ourselves personally. This teaching has influenced many
writings. Instead of generalizing in order to embrace
more and more people, many authors particularize to
the personal to make contact with the deeper areas of
the lives of readers. I have found this to be a profitable
approach particularly when speaking or writing about
the work of the Spirit of God in our lives. I believe that
by sharing with you my personal life and reflections and
how I have experienced the generous love of God, I can
communicate a deeper sense of what charismatic renewal is about. My purpose is to communicate what was
news and good to me in the hope that it will be good
news to you or at least that it will enable you to understand your fellow Catholics who now suddenly
punctuate sentences with "Praise the Lord."

The charismatic renewal is certainly not the only renewal in the Catholic Church. We have experienced the
scriptural and liturgical renewals which grew in popularity immediately following the Second Vatican Council. We know of the Cursillo, the Catholic Family Movement, Marriage Encounter, Better World Movement and
Focolare. Even if we are not familiar with the nature of
these movements, we will recognize their effects in such
changes as Mass in English, congregational singing,
communion in the hand, married people approaching
communion as a couple, preaching that analyzes the
cultural situation in which a scriptural event took place
and the emphasis on Christ as an elder brother.

This book, however, confines itself to the charismatic
renewal, and in particular the Catholic Charismatic Re-

newal. It treats the renewal in direct relationship to the Church it is designed to renew. It is crucial to understand that the charismatic renewal is designed to disappear into a renewed church. It is also crucial to understand that the charismatic renewal does not purport to offer the Church anything new; it contends only that God is calling attention to what was in the center of the life of the Church for centuries but which has been overlooked or greatly undervalued in the modern church. Because of what the Lord is doing today, we are rediscovering as real, life-giving and empowering the basic gifts of God born of the Spirit in the heart of the Church. This is the contention of the charismatic renewal and the central concern of this book.

CHAPTER ONE

BEGINNINGS

At Duquesne University in Pittsburgh, a group of students had met regularly with several professors to study Scripture and to pray. After two years of such meetings the group, known as the Chi-Rho Society, agreed to make a retreat weekend together. This was before February, 1967.

One professor, Dr. William Storey, asked the students at the beginning of the retreat: "Are you ready for what the Spirit of God can do in your life?" As the weekend progressed, many knew they were being confronted with what it would mean to surrender fully to the Lord. As Patti Gallagher Mansfield, then a student, recounted: "Jesus was asking us to let him reign, not simply to acknowledge him as an important person, but to allow him into the very center of our lives."[1] Patti continued:

That Saturday evening, Feb. 18, 1967, was an important night in my life and in the Catholic Charismatic Renewal. During a birthday party at the retreat, I wandered up into the chapel to see if any of my friends were there. I

[1] Ralph Martin (Compiler). *The Spirit and the Church*, New York: Paulist Press, 1976, p. 5.

didn't plan on praying myself. I was simply going to call my friends down to the party.

But as I entered and knelt in the presence of the Lord in the Blessed Sacrament, I trembled with the awareness that it was God himself, in all his holiness, before whom I had come. I found myself praying from the depths of my being a prayer of total surrender to the Lord. "Yes, your will be done. I accept whatever it will mean to follow you. Only teach me how to love."

In the next few moments I found myself prostrate before the altar and filled with an awareness of God's personal love for me: a love that is so completely undeserved, so utterly foolish, so lavishly given. The only word that came to my mind in those moments was "stay." I often think of Augustine's prayer when recalling that night. "You have made us for yourself, O Lord, and there is no rest until we rest in you."

Even though I wanted to remain in the chapel and enjoy the presence of the Lord there and within me, I knew that what I had experienced was meant to be shared. Without fully understanding what had happened, I was convinced that God intended for all his people to know his love and presence in a deep, personal way.

I left the chapel and told our Chaplain what I had just experienced. I learned from him that David Mangan had just been in the chapel an hour before. Dave, also, had encountered the Lord in a more powerful way than ever before. I asked this priest which people I should tell about what had happened, and he simply said that the Lord would show me. How often those words have echoed in my ears, "The Lord will show you," as the Lord has led me to share his love with brothers and sisters from different parts of the country and the world.

Before the end of the party, all the students were

drawn into the chapel. It was as though Jesus were walking among us as we knelt there and touching each person
in some special way. Some said they experienced a deep
peace or joy or the desire to praise God. We didn't fully
understand that what was happening among us was a
release of the power of God's Spirit and that we would
become known as the first Catholic Charismatic prayer
group.[2]

In the weeks and months following that retreat
weekend, God's Spirit was lavish in their lives. The gifts
of the Spirit described in 1 Cor. 12 were poured out upon
them: some praised God in tongues; some were healed;
Scripture came alive in power; the courage to witness to
Jesus Christ grew among them.

In retrospect these Christian men and women realized
that while they had loved the Lord, prayed and desired
to serve him, nevertheless, loving Him and being fully
surrendered to Him were two different things; that
prayer under our will power and with the best of intentions was still vastly different from prayer in the conscious experienced power of the Holy Spirit; that the
charity they practiced toward others was laudable but
the unity of brothers and sisters brought about by the
Spirit which enabled them to proclaim Jesus with
power in serving others was beyond comparison.

Others came to visit these professors and students,
and pray with them including Ralph Martin, Steve
Clark, Gerry Rauch and Jim Cavnar. Ralph and Steve,
at that point, were national leaders in the Cursillo
movement. When these men had been prayed with for a
deeper outpouring of the Spirit, they returned to Notre
Dame, to Michigan State and the charismatic renewal
began to spread. First, it was students but quickly

[2]*Ibid.*, p. 6–7.

people from all walks of life,[3] all ages began to pray for the release of the full power of the Holy Spirit already within them through the Sacraments of Baptism and Confirmation and to know their inheritance as sons and daughters of God.

These small beginnings formed the base for a renewal within the Catholic Church involving hundreds of thousands of people in the United States and around the world over the past twelve years. Those of us in the renewal do believe that the present outpouring of the Spirit is the direct intervention of the merciful love of God in our human history. God is lavishing upon all of his people who seek it that portion of our inheritance which Paul speaks about in Romans. For many on the original Duquesne weekend, the experience was not a temporary one but one which permanently affected their Christian commitment. David Mangan and his wife are now members of the The Word of God Community in Ann Arbor, Michigan. Karina Sefcik Treiber is Director of Career Planning at the College of Steubenville, Steubenville, Ohio and a member of the Servants of God's Love, a Catholic covenant community, Steubenville, Ohio. Gerry and Annamarie Cafardi teach in a Christian High School, the Word of God Academy in Erie, Pennsylvania. Len and Elaine Ransil teach in the same Christian school. Patti Gallagher Mansfield is a member of a covenant community, the Community of Jesus the King in New Orleans, Louisiana and is the wife of a coordinator in that community. Mary Beth Mutmansky is a member of the Community of God's Love,

---

[3] Among the pioneers at Notre Dame were Kevin Ranaghan, now Director of the National Communications Office for the Catholic Charismatic Renewal and his wife, Dorothy. Both Kevin and Dorothy are now members of the National Service Committee for Catholic Charismatic Renewal in the United States.

Rutherford, New Jersey. A number of other students quickly followed the example of those on the original Duquesne weekend. To mention a few, Bert Ghezzi is now a coordinator in The Word of God Community in Ann Arbor, Michigan and the Editor of *New Covenant* Magazine. John Burt is Director of Admissions at the College of Steubenville, Steubenville, Ohio and a member of the Servants of God's Love Community. Jack Flanagan is Assistant Director of Admissions at the College of Steubenville and is a pastoral leader in the Servants of God's Love Community.

The Spirit of God has turned many of us in the renewal upside down, inside out, changed our plans, our futures, our very lives. Many of us have begun to glimpse a portion of God's plan for his people—His Church:

- —where people know they are personally loved and cared for by the Lord and one another;
- —where the power of the Spirit leads to personal conversion and a laying down of life to care for brothers and sisters;
- —where future priests are called forth from an already established faith community to prepare to shepherd that community;
- —where authority is experienced as life-giving and freeing;
- —where all vocations, all states of life find their direction, support and nourishment from a Christian community of men and women committed to Jesus Christ as Lord;
- —where those committed relationships enable men and women to hear the Gospel mandate as Good News and know the power to witness to others that same Good News;

—where the liturgical and sacramental life of the Church is fully alive because that life is being celebrated as it was intended—among committed brothers and sisters in Jesus Christ.

I first began to understand pastorally what the universal church alive could be when I participated in the International Catholic Charismatic Congress in Rome, Italy, May, 1975. The liturgical celebrations with Pope Paul VI as chief celebrant on Pentecost Sunday, with Cardinal Suenens as celebrant at the High Altar in St. Peter's Basilica on Pentecost Monday, and the audience with Pope Paul VI were some of the highlights of that conference. Even now I can recall those days vividly. . . .

It was a beautiful Saturday morning as we left Pacem in Terris, the place where I resided, for the catacombs. The bus was filled with excited joyful people. It had to be an historic day. In the morning we had workshops. I was assigned to one of four tents raised for the conference. Our tent was filled with excited people desirous of hearing how the sacraments were integrated into charismatic renewal. They were Catholics alive with the Holy Spirit and deeply committed to the sacraments which had nourished their faith for many years. The talk went well. The people responded enthusiastically to my statements on how the celebration of the sacraments could and should be renewed. Father Serafino Falvo translated my talk into Italian. He did it with such gusto and humor that he added immensely to the occasion. It was a delightful time for everyone.

That afternoon I was chairman of the main session. I had agreed to lead the assembly of over ten thousand from approximately fifty nations in a renewal of their baptism and confirmation. I had assistants, Father

Jean-Michael Garrigues, French, Father Salvador Carillo, Spanish, Father Serafino Falvo, Italian and Father Heribert Mühlen, German, who were to provide a free translation to my remarks. After an initial time of praise and song, I gave my presentation, probably fifteen minutes in length. The four translators averaged ten minutes each. At the end of the last talk there was a clear restlessness in the gathering. The uniqueness of the occasion could no longer hold the attention of those present. Hearing the same message in five languages had been a strain. Something new was needed. I began to receive numerous notes suggesting various courses of action. One called for silence, another for loud praise. One proposed a song by the music ministry, another a simple musical refrain that everyone could sing. Some had scripture passages to be read, others wanted personal testimonies. I informed the leaders that we would wait to determine what the *Lord* was calling us to do. As we sat in silence, I received a strong impression that the Lord wanted me to look at his people and see what he was doing among them. As I looked out upon this amazing assembly of people from all over the world, gathered in this field above the catacombs, I saw in them the desire to be one. They yearned to celebrate what they had in common with one another.

I stood and asked them to greet and embrace all around them those who did not speak their language. There was an immediate response. They rushed into each other's arms. They laughed and hugged and cried as Frenchman and Puerto Rican embraced, as Englishman and German greeted one another, as Oriental, Arab, South African and American gave each other a greeting of peace. Looks and gestures predominated as few present could communicate in words to their foreign brothers and sisters. We celebrated what I had spoken of earlier in the session: that the Body of Christ was the central reality of life, not national language or culture. We were first of all Christians together and we lived by the same Spirit, the power which had conquered the world. In celebration of this message, the gathering cheered, sang and danced. The joy exploded and the unplanned celebration extended far beyond anything we had seen in the renewal to that date. When the bishops on the platform started to dance, the gathering responded with shouts of approval and general glee. The celebration exceeded what anyone had anticipated. We were singing and dancing not just anywhere but in Rome and with the bishops and atop the Catacombs and with brothers and sisters we normally ignored because we couldn't speak the language. Truly it was Catholic— the celebration that the Church is universal but one, varied but united. We continued, expecting that the enthusiasm would fall off. It didn't; if anything, it grew, but many minutes later fatigue began to take its toll and I called the assembly to quiet. We prayed then, laying hands on one another that we might be empowered to live out in our local situation what we had celebrated that day: to live a renewed life, in union with brothers and sisters—to lay aside forever the national, political and cultural barriers that separate and divide even Catholics from one another.

The following day was another high point in the Conference program as all ten thousand converged on St. Peter's for the celebration of the Pentecost liturgy by Pope Paul VI.

It was a bright May morning. The blue sky gave promise to a day that would parallel the beauty and expectation already in the hearts of ten thousand people. There was an overwhelming awe about it all, an awe that we might be privileged to be there, an awe that there were so many others, so many brothers and sisters from around the world who had the same desires in their hearts as we did, desires to love and serve the Lord, desires to be more and more on fire with His Holy Spirit, desires to be more and more deeply empowered to serve the coming of the Kingdom of God.

As we gathered that morning, we spoke in many languages. We had many diverse ways of approaching things, but we had one mind and one heart. There were many others also gathered in the Basilica to celebrate that Liturgy from many, many parts of the world. There was a whole African delegation of about five or six hundred. They were dressed in their African tribal garb and added a splendor and a beauty to what God was about as He brought us all together.

When the Pope finally came in, the Sistine Choir began to sing the processional. When they completed it, softly in the background you could begin to hear the eight-fold "Alleluia," ten thousand voices singing it softly but still exultantly.

In his homily the Holy Father spoke of a call to rejoicing. He told us that the kind of exuberant enthusiasm that St. Peter had on the day of Pentecost gives the Church a revelation of the inner life of the Trinity. He said that, if we comprehend the Church's doctrine on the Holy Spirit, we would want not only to possess the Holy Spirit but to experience the sensible effects of His presence within us. For we know the Spirit is light, strength, charism, infusion of superior vitality, virtues, gifts and fruits. The Pope then gave a description of the activity of the Holy Spirit which is close to the charismatic renewal's description of being baptized in the Holy Spirit. He said,

The Holy Spirit, that is God-Love, lives in the soul and the soul suddenly feels itself invaded by a need to abandon itself to love and it is aware of a surprising and unusual courage that makes it joyful and secure. A courage to speak . . . to sing . . . to proclaim to others . . . all the wonderful works of God.

During the Mass as the Holy Father consecrated the bread, raised it for all to see, there was a hushed but audible singing in tongues, harmony that was truly unearthly. Again it happened; the Holy Father raised the chalice and he held it there for what seemed an extended period of time, until the voices that sung in unearthly harmony faded into silence . . . into a silence of worship and adoration. At Communion I was privileged to receive Holy Communion from the Holy Father. As I moved closer toward him, there was a deep sense in me of how much this man bore for me . . . what a burden he was carrying for me and for all of my brothers and sisters. A gratitude welled up in my heart that I could not describe. I found myself simply praying for him and as I received Communion from him I looked into his eyes that burned; there is no other way to describe them . . . burned with a love. I grew in a compassion and in an understanding for him who represents Our Father in Heaven.

When the Liturgy was over, the Sistine Choir attempted a recessional but by then, joyful and exultant voices were singing again the eight-fold "Alleluia," the one song that we could all sing in the same language . . . the one song that we were all certain of and that expressed the exuberance and joy and hope and faith that was in our hearts that day. And we sang it until finally the Sistine Choir and the organ stopped and they joined us. What a day it was! What a glory it was! God, our God, was with us. The Spirit of God really hovered over us . . . the Spirit of God who truly sought to make us one . . . was doing that.

The following day on Pentecost Monday, Cardinal Suenens was given the unusual privilege of celebrating the Mass at the High Altar which is usually reserved for the Pope alone. But Pope Paul as a beautiful gesture had given him permission to celebrate Mass from that altar. He and seven hundred other priests gathered again in a joyful celebration that was now all ours . . . all ten thousand of us gathered together. Beside us were Africans and Frenchmen, Spaniards and Portuguese, Germans, Australians, all the peoples of the world. We gathered together to praise and glorify our God. The conclusion of that Liturgy, the time after Communion, the Lord spoke to us in great power. He told us of difficult days and difficult times ahead. He told us that things would not be easy for us. He told us that we would suffer for him, but he told us that he was beginning to work in a new way . . . and that he was exhorting us to trust more deeply in him. He was promising us that Christ himself would be our joy. He would be our comfort and he would be our deliverance in the midst of suffering.

At the conclusion of that liturgy, all of us quietly prayed and sang for a half hour, awaiting the arrival of Pope Paul and an audience that we were privileged to have with him. When he appeared, everyone again began to sing spontaneously "Alleluia"; it was a joyful song. And the Holy Father seemed to respond to us with smiles and waving and we were deeply touched. The Pope, first of all, read a message to us in French, then gave summaries in Spanish and English. He spoke to us with open encouragement. He commented on the necessity for spiritual renewal for modern men who imagine that they are rulers of their own destiny. He expressed a warm appreciation for an experience, a personal relationship with God, which is typical of the renewal. He developed three Scriptural guidelines and he said to us that if we adhered to them, then we would be assured that the renewal would not veer into error and that it would make a sound contribution to the renewal of the whole church. All three principles we find in the letter to Paul. The first is: fidelity to the true doctrine of the faith; secondly, seeking the higher gifts which build up the community of the faithful; finally the supremacy of love which is the way of Christian perfection and the necessary context for the use of the spiritual gifts.

After he completed this prepared statement, he addressed a personal word of support to the charismatic renewal.

> Your spiritual renewal ought to rejuvenate the world, give it back a spirituality, a soul, a religious thought. The renewal ought to open the world's closed lips to pray and open its mouth to song, to joy, to hymns, and to witnessing.

He directed a special word to the pilgrims present in the Basilica who were not part of the conference, calling them to participate in spiritual renewal. As the Pope spoke, his voice grew more and more vibrant and as he ended, he cried out, "Jesus is Lord, Alleluia!" (Full Text of the Holy Father's talk can be found on p. 153.)

For all of us, it was a moving moment: to know that we had a father here on earth who so cared for us, who was so guiding us, leading us. And so many of us felt a deeper need than ever before to pray for him to support him in every way that we could. When the Pope left, again, everyone sang the eight-fold "Alleluia" with a harmony, with accents—there were many accents—but the voices were all in many-splendored harmony that had a foretaste of the unity that God desires for his people.

We moved out into the square and began to dance our joy, our joy that we had a Father in Heaven, a joy that we had known the power of the Spirit, our joy that we had a Church that had absorbed us and embraced us and gathered us to herself.

We had begun to experience the beginnings of a Church alive. The work was ahead of us in our local areas around the world but we had glimpsed a vision of what could be.

How had we gotten from Duquesne to Rome? What had happened in the hearts of people over eight years, that from a small group of students we would grow to the Ninth International Conference comprising ten thousand people, maximum registration permitted, from fifty nations.

Perhaps that question is best answered by telling you my own story. While some events and circumstances and places change, the story for hundreds of thousands of people is the same in its basic thrust: I was hungry to know the Lord Jesus more fully in my life. The Lord responded with the power of his Spirit.

Pope Paul's audience with Charismatics in Rome for the International Conference for Charismatic Renewal among Catholics. It was held over Pentecost weekend, May, 1975.

Reading of the Scriptures at Charismatic Mass in St. Peter's in Rome, 1975. Cardinal Suenens was principal celebrant. Dr. Kevin Ranaghan is the deacon proclaiming the Word of God.

Word of God Music Ministry from Word of God Community in Ann Arbor, Mich. It led the 10,000 participants in the Rome conference in song.

Dancing in a field at the Rome conference of 1975.

Photos: New Covenant Magazine

cle by Vinson Synan

July, 1975. pp. 44-46

Pentecost in St. Peter'

Pentecost Sunday, 1975, will
church history
Zealandia. The Catholic Sunday Paper, June 8, 1975, P. 9

Vatican views Charismatic Renewal

by John

ABC, Madrid, May 21, 1975

Without giving an explicit green
all elements n the charismatic
Vatican has clearly indicated that a move-
of the bishops could only be

One of NC Ne
time journalists
who filed thi
on the recent
tional meeting c
charismatics in

PABLO VI RECIB
PEDRO A DIEZ M
SENTANTES DE LO
CARISMATICOS C.

Ciudad del Vaticano

OSV
Aug 7
p. 2

Vatican cautious but hopeful concerning the future of Catholic Charismatics

By Charles Savitsky
OSV Rome correspondent

a certain friendliness toward the Ch
matics.

TICAN CITY (OSV
arismatic m
garo, May 24-25, 1975, p. 14

The
he (

The Pilot, Boston

Rome :

"Test Everything, Keeping That Which is Good

ophéties et guérisons
grand nombre
congrès néo-pentecô

me, 23 mai (De notre en
special)
Le congrès charismatique de
laissé un impact plus

ces · et son habit bla
cain.

Son · atelier · a é
quente durant le c
ne femme l'arrête

Pope Hails Signs of Fa In 'Charismatic' Rene

By John Mu

6 Part IV – Sun, June 8, 1975

More About Pentecosta

enst, Herder Freiburg und Wein, 1. Halbjahr, 1975

Urchristliche Charismen im Petersdom

— Heribert Mühler

dem Schlußgottesdienst, den die etwa 10000 Teilnehmer an dem
alen Pfingst-Kongreß der katholisch-charismati
erung in Rom zusammen mit etwa 40000
fragten einige der anwesenden
Ein bekannter Profes
nglaublich! (

St. Louis Review, August 8, 1975

Los Angeles Times
Page One lead story this w
Charismatic Clai
page is a
celebr

Charismatics Gain Pope's

Controver
Catholic Movement Blessed Du

BY R

e Reportedly Supports Charismatics

servers from non-Catholic Churches that he en
countered in Rome.
ther Fullam said that the Pope, ending his
with a ringing acclamation familiar to
the Lord, Alleluia
the movement

Protestant observers included Dr. J.
man Williams, president of Melo-
d School of Theology in An-
and the Rev. Louis P. Shel-
inistrator of the new charis-
ool.

ccasion portended an
breakthrough in the
church," commented
er of a continuing di-
ismatic movement
Protestant and

The setting
the conferen
St. Callixtus,
many martyrs
tent, seating 8,0
ries, workshop
Dr. Williams du
here last week,
ing sense of God
somehow as

martyrs

Mr. Shel
storic

mpo, Saturday, May 17, p. 21

OMA IL CONGRESSO DEL NUOVO MOVIMENTO RELIGIOS

Vision Magazine, Australia, July-August,

mistero dei

‹carismati

dottrina nata nel 1967
l'Università di Duquesne

Festival of J

The Rev. Alan Langstaff reports on t
Catholic Charismatic Conference in Rome.
God's grace", said Brian Smith,
wal Services, that a
al commenc

PERSONAL WITNESS

I knew it was a decisive moment in my life as I sat at my desk that Wednesday morning in October of 1969. The night before I had been prayed with to be baptized in the Holy Spirit. In the ensuing twelve hours, I continually experienced the presence of God in a new way. First, I was drawn into a deep still awareness of being caught up in God in a new way. Then, after about an hour I was aware of a new power to pray, and a new means of prayer through the language of tongues. Then, through the night, I awoke regularly to realize that the praise of God was going on in me. I wasn't praying; I was caught up in the prayer of the Trinity. When I arose in the morning, this prayer continued in a more expressive way. Now, the last hour, I had read the New Testament and found more power and more immediacy to the words than I had known before. The Acts of the Apostles seemed to be about *my* life; they reflected what I was experiencing. The Spirit within me jumped as I read and my strongest desire was to read Scripture all day and night.

I knew it was a time for decision what I would do about all of this. I was Rector President of St. Francis

Major Seminary, a seminary serving fourteen different dioceses. I had to communicate regularly with the fourteen bishops who sent men to our seminary. I was Superior of the Franciscan Monastery. I did have a vicar superior who handled the day to day business of the house, but I had the responsibility to see that everything was carried out in good order in accord with the Franciscan Rule and Constitution. I also served as definitor of our Provincial Curia, the six-man policy making body of our Franciscan Province and as Vice Chairman of the Board of Trustees of St. Francis College. Suddenly, these appointments which had seemed so promising when they were made, took on a heaviness. What would be the response of the bishops, the seminarians, the Franciscan clerics, the seminary faculty and the trustees of the College if I took on a new way of charismatic or Pentecostal living? I had a reputation for prudence, administrative efficiency and "enlightened theology." Certainly what I was now experiencing would seem to many to be incompatible with such a reputation. I sat still for a long time and reflected on the events of my life which had brought me to this moment.

I was born in Far Rockaway, New York and spent my first seven years in the apartment house owned by my father in Cedarhurst, New York. Following my parents' divorce, my mother and I moved in with my grandparents. I went off to Catholic boarding schools. Five years at Coindre Hall in Huntington, New York under the Brothers of the Sacred Heart taught me a discipline of study and desire for personal integrity which would stay with me throughout the intervening years. In elementary school I did everything: played all sports, competed with two of my friends for first in class, went to Mass daily, was Chairman of the Spiritual Committee of our Sodality and became Librarian of our school library. By the time I was graduating from Coindre Hall, my mother had decided to remarry, this time to a Protestant who seriously opposed much of Catholic doctrine and practice. I went off on a scholarship to New Hampton School in New Hampshire. At least twice a week we had a Congregationalist Chapel service. I never understood the service, though I recognized it as greatly different from the Catholic Mass. After four years at New Hampton, I graduated salutatorian and winner of the coveted Study, Sport, Spirit medal.

As I entered Williams College in Massachusetts, I was a Sunday Catholic whose greatest desire was to be popular. I joined the most popular fraternity and engaged in all the sports, practices and activities of fraternity life. My life took on a pattern of averageness. I sought out the "gentleman's life" of just enough academics, co-curricular activities. I occasionally drank too much, bragged too much and played cards too much. But on the whole I wasn't distinguishing myself in anything. During the summer between my freshman and sophomore years, I served for three months as a deckhand in the merchant marine. My two bunkmates had served time in the federal penitentary and constantly pressured me to join them in drink, sex, gambling or cheating. For the first time I had to stand alone and say "no," though I flirted with many compromises.

In my sophomore year I took a basic Philosophy course which challenged me as to what I believed. I became aware that I had to choose a set of beliefs. I couldn't take my beliefs from my family, my church, my friends or my teachers. I had to decide for myself and treat as my own a system of beliefs about all of reality. I was shaken by this. For the first time, I speculated that God may not exist, that Christianity might be a farce and that what I held as goodness might not be goodness at all. I looked for a time to resolve this. I decided to take my birthday, December 1, 1950, and seek basic truth. I left the dormitory at dawn and went into the woods. I reasoned and reasoned on philosophical principles and I prayed to God that, if He existed, he would reveal the truth to me. By midafternoon I was certain God existed and I began to seek from God the truth about the universe, about Jesus Christ and about the Catholic Church. At ten o'clock that night, I emerged from the woods knowing that certain doctrines were true for me and always would be true. God existed and was in control, he heard and responded to prayer, Jesus was his Son both God and Man, Jesus had established a Church to be truth-telling and life-transmitting so that all mankind could find salvation and understanding and I was called to serve in that Church. Every year since, I have set aside special time on my birthday to thank God for my nineteenth birthday gift.

There were some immediate changes in my life. I recognized that I now stood for something and that I couldn't agree with many things said and done by my friends. Others recognized a change in me. I was elected Secretary of the Newman Club, the Catholic society at the College. In Public Speaking class the professor regularly asked me to take positions defending Christianity or the Catholic Church. My fraternity brothers began to exclude me from some events which they presumed I would consider immoral. In my junior year I was elected President of the Newman Club, Rushing Chairman of the Fraternity and an editor of two college publications. I knew these positions came out of respect for me and not from popularity.

The following summer I entered a serious relationship with a girl. We grew in love for one another and began moving toward marriage. She was a year behind me so, as she entered her senior year in a woman's college, I was entering my first year at Harvard Law School. I had chosen law because I desired to know much more about life before I settled on a career. I chose Harvard because I understood it to be the most difficult challenge. I was able to gain acceptance because of good grades in my last two years plus a surprisingly high score on the Law School Aptitude Test.

During my first year at Harvard Law, I was caught up in the intense competition of both the classes and world of law. I thrilled to the battle and experienced the adage that "the law was my mistress." I resented anyone who would draw me away from my studies. Understandably this strained the relationship with the woman I was to marry. Nothing existed but law and succeeding. My classes formed me in winning, not in striving to be right. There was a growing emptiness in me and when Ash Wednesday came, I decided to renew my commitment to God. I elected to do it with prayer at sunrise, daily Mass and fasting. The effect was overwhelming to me. God was present to me, I was actually walking each day with Him to and from the Church. I committed my whole life to Him and heard Him call me into fulltime service. I begged Him to let me complete my present task, then, I would come. It seemed to me that He agreed. I summed up the contract saying, "God, if you will stand back for a time so that I can graduate from law school and pass the bar exam and therefore make my family happy, I will then go anywhere and do anything in your service." Easter was glorious, I knew a new peace with God. I completed the year successfully and terminated my relationship with the girl I was to marry. She rightly had called for marriage, now or never, and I chose the latter. I worked that summer as a night elevator operator. This continued a unusual pattern of summer jobs such as taxi driver, handyman at a woman's vacation camp, tennis court manager, golf caddy and of course, deckhand in the merchant marine.

The next two years of law school went quickly. I continued to enjoy the competition. I made an agreement with a good friend: he made all the arrangements for our weekened social life and I controlled the schedule of our week long academic life. I became Rushing Chairman of Lincoln's Inn, the exclusive social society at Harvard Law. I was living in the mainstream of student life, but I never forgot my agreement with God. During Lent, 1955 and 1956, I repeated my pattern of commitment with special fasting and daily Mass.

During the summer of 1955 I served as a student assistant in the United States Attorney's Office for the Southern District of New York. I thrilled to the practice of courtroom law in the Criminal Division to which I was assigned. In the Fall I renewed my dedication to the Harvard Voluntary Defenders which assisted the Public Defender of Boston. My final year at law school passed easily. I was confident of my ability and I was also resigned to being less than a legal genius. I graduated in the top fourth of my class. I received many offers from law firms and chose a prestigious firm on Wall Street.

Along with many of my classmates we rushed from our last exam to take a "cram course" for the New York Bar Exam. This course was necessary to learn the procedures and rules peculiar to the state jurisdiction of New York. I enjoyed the intense studying which varied from ten to fourteen hours a day. I knew great peace in taking this exam but many of my friends suffered hypertension. Two thirds of those taking the exam failed it each year. Failure could shipwreck a legal career. Furthermore it would be almost five months before the results of the exam were published. Within days after taking the two day exam, I entered active duty as an Air Force First Lieutenant stationed at Andrews Air Force Base. Looking back now, I can see the conflicts between my commitment for full time service to God, my accepting a position in a law firm and my going on active duty with the Air Force. But, at the same time I sensed that it would all work out.

Through an unusual series of events I was appointed Staff Judge Advocate of the 85th Air Division at Andrews. I was the chief legal officer for units on bases from Delaware to North Carolina. I enjoyed the challenges both in and out of the courtroom.

In October, 1956, while I was on temporary duty at Stewart Air Force Base in Newburgh, New York, the announcement appeared that the New York Bar Exam results were published in the *New York Times*. A few of my friends ran up to me carrying the newspaper and shouting, "Mike, you made it!" There were immediate plans for celebration, but I experienced a spiritual tug. I went to my room, knelt down and said, "OK, God, I'm yours." Immediately there was a rush of spiritual excitement in me and I sensed the words, "I want you to be a priest in a religious order." I said yes and suddenly, the Air Force and the Wall Street law firm disappeared from importance.

I immediately began investigating religious orders and preparing for seminary studies. I visited the Jesuits, Dominicans and Franciscans. Father Avery Dulles, S.J., directed me that "a vocation is the restless Spirit of God with you. When that Spirit settles and is at home, stop and join the group where you are." The Spirit settled in Loretto, Pa. on a visit to the Franciscans of the Third Order Regular, I joined up.

I continued in my legal work as a Judge Advocate and experienced some success in the courtroom. I won my first five cases and was sought after by airmen accused of serious crime.

In the meantime, I was being tutored in Latin twice a week, reading spiritual manuals and participating in all base chapel activities. The most vibrant gathering in the base chapel was the Monday night novena to Our Lady of Perpetual Help. My faith was built up each week at this novena. The preaching centered on God's desire to meet all our needs and here, this regularly happened through the intercession of Mary. When we met on December 24, 1956, Chaplain Finke announced to us that the next novena meeting would be held as usual on Monday, December 31st, New Year's Eve. He knew most of us would be going to a New Year's Eve party that night and, though he was prepared for the worst in attendance, he didn't see why we couldn't bring our dates to the novena before going to the party.

I spoke with a nurse who attended the novena and dated a friend of mine. We both decided to ask our dates to come to the novena. On New Year's Eve when Chaplain Finke genuflected before the altar and in a discouraging fashion turned to the congregation, he saw the largest group ever assembled for a devotional service. Most of us were in black tie with our dates in evening gowns, but we were there smiling at him. He prayed for a moment and said, "I believe God wants to give you a special gift. I want each person here to ask for something important for your life, something you haven't asked for before and ask that you receive it before the end of 1957." As I prayed, I knew the desire of my heart: I asked to be in a religious order by September, almost a year before I was scheduled for discharge from the Air Force. Joyce the nurse, asked to be able to marry Ernie, her date. Ernie asked to come back to the Catholic Church from which he had totally absented himself for many years. In April, 1957 I was best man at Joyce and Ernie's wedding; Ernie had been a daily communicant for three months. In September, Joyce and Ernie bid me goodbye as I left on an unexpected early discharge from the Air Force. The next time I would see them would be my First Mass celebrated as a priest in May, 1964.

It was difficult to tell my mother and father about my decision. They were disappointed; my mother wanted grandchildren and my father had counted on me being a successful lawyer. They grew to accept the decision as they experienced the beauty of Franciscan life. I never doubted the rightness of my calling to the Franciscan priesthood. The seven years of study and spiritual formation were filled with peace and happiness. My mother, her final years marked with the signs of sanctity, died before I completed my studies and my father died three years after my ordination.

I was invigorated by the new theology emerging from the Vatican Council. I continued to deepen in my love for the ideals of St. Francis and I learned to treasure daily meditation. My ordination and First Mass were beautiful experiences of God's love. I was excited to be a priest. After ordination I was assigned to the College of Steubenville where I was a lecturer in theology, director of the honors program and Dean of the College. I became deeply involved in the Cursillo Movement which centered on a three day intense course in Christian life and leadership. I had found in the Cursillo a new awareness of Jesus as our brother and the joy of celebrating that. I also dedicated myself to the causes of social justice and struggled with compassion and anger, particularly as I wrestled with the issues of "black power." It was so difficult for me to separate the good causes from some violent means. I learned to love and respect my black friends so much that I deeply missed them in an absence from Steubenville. Subsequently, I learned to love many of the dedicated leaders of the peace movement, but through it all I sensed the inadequacy of their programs to build a just society.

In August, 1969, I was elected to the Provincial Curia and to the twin positions of Rector and Superior at St. Francis Seminary. Suddenly, I realized that I didn't have the spiritual resources to discharge my responsibilities. I didn't know how to lead seminarians to holiness; I wasn't able to set the example they needed. I experienced an emptiness and a frustration. When it came to holiness, what could I do? This was so much more than a position calling for administrative skills and theological competence. I spoke of this to the person whose holiness I most respected, the Superior of the Discalced Carmelite Sisters, cloistered in a monastery in Loretto. Sister Caroline heard me out and said, "Mike, what you need is the Baptism of the Spirit." In response to my question, "What is it?", she told me of a recent meeting with Father Francis MacNutt, O.P., who prayed with her to be baptized in the Holy Spirit. She told me of a new intimacy with God, a new power to love and a new way to praise God. I trusted her and the affirmation of my own spirit, so as to say, "Will you pray with me that I may receive it?" She responded, "No, you need an expert." I began to seek my expert.

When the new seminarians arrived, one of them was Bob Conlin, a man in his mid-twenties who was involved in the charismatic renewal. Bob kept me informed of the developments in the renewal and assured me that Father Jim Ferry, a priest of the Newark Diocese, would pray with me when he came to give a lecture at Saint Francis College, also in Loretto, in October. In the meantime, Father Roland Faley, T.O.R., the former rector and my spiritual director for years, encouraged me to look into this new spiritual development in the Church.

When the night of Jim Ferry's talk came, I was ready. I had experienced two months of difficult problems in directing the seminary. I needed what only God could give. I went to the lecture with most of my seminary faculty. As Jim and a young graduate student, Joe Breault, who accompanied him, spoke of Jesus, my spirit leaped as it had done that day Sister Caroline told me of being baptized in the Spirit. A spiritual pressure grew inside me and I became impatient for the gift I so needed. I actively participated in the discussion, witnessing to God's faithfulness in my life. There followed a session of informal discussion and, finally, a time of prayer. Jim asked if anyone wanted to pray for anything. There was a pause in the group of college and seminary students and faculty, then I went down on my knees in the center of the ring of chairs and said, "Yes, to be baptized in the Holy Spirit." Jim directed everyone to pray for me and many students and faculty placed their trembling hands on me; they knew less than I did what was transpiring.

I don't remember the prayer. I know only that God took over. I had spent many retreats seeking God's presence through contemplative prayer. I had regularly sought out times each week and days each year for extended prayer. I had been to the Trappists in Gethsemane and other contemplative houses for growth in prayer but in that moment, God grasped me up into Himself. I wanted nothing else; I desired to be lost in God, the fullness of life. I knew the intimacy of union in love. I remained kneeling, lost in what was happening. Someone moved me to a corner where I continued in prayer for an unknown period of time. Then, I felt a tap on my shoulder and someone informed me that we were going to pray for a gift of wisdom for one of the priests present. I walked over to the group and started to pray aloud a prayer of petition. The words came out jumbled, not the English words I intended. I tried again and again, they were jumbled. I kept silent and reflected on the experience. I realized that I must be experiencing the "gift of tongues," a way of praise and prayer that was common among those who had been baptized in the Spirit. Just before going to bed that night, I whispered to Jim Ferry about what had happened. He replied that I had received the gift and I should regularly use it in prayer.

After reflecting back over my life, I knew it was time for a decision. What had happened to me in the last twelve hours? The answer came clear and I wrote down on my pad: "I know the presence of the Risen Lord Jesus as I have never known it before." The key word was "Risen." There was a presence of the Glorified Jesus such as I never knew was possible. Suddenly, I was sharing in the truth that the crucifixion and death was over and past. What was now present was a risen glorified life given to me. I wrote further, "I can never deny the truth of what has happened." I knew I would be tempted to deny it in difficult times so I steeled my mind to this resolution. I resolved to research everything I could about the Pentecostal Experience and the charismatic renewal. I contacted Jim Ferry and Bob Conlin and obtained books and tapes. I spent hours each day in research. When I learned that I was the only priest in Pennsylvania known to be involved in charismatic renewal, I doubled my efforts to find all the answers.

My closest friends in the Franciscans heard that something had happened to me and began probing. My answers surprised all but one, Father David Tickerhoof.

Dave began fasting and preparing. He came to the seminary to hear Ralph Martin from The Word of God Charismatic Community in Ann Arbor. After Ralph's talk, we prayed for Dave and he experienced God with similar power to what had happened to me.

About the same time I met Father Francis MacNutt, O.P., at a Full Gospel Businessmen's dinner in the Pittsburgh area. Francis and I became close friends and soon were giving talks together and ministering God's healing power. Francis taught me a great deal and I developed it in a sacramental and communal context, first writing *the Power of Penance* on the Sacrament of Reconciliation, then *Inner Healing*, which developed the first book, then with Sister Ann Shields, R.S.M., *and Their Eyes Were Opened: Encountering Jesus in the Sacraments.* Steve Clark[1] became my main resource for understanding community and Kevin Ranaghan for deepening my theology of sacraments.

I began to experience new courage and love within me. This was most evident when I became aware of the unlawful means the Attorney General's office was using to prosecute the Berrigans. Though I didn't agree with all the Berrigans were doing, I went to Harrisburg, Pa. and conducted a workshop on the legality of the government's prosecution. I subsequently gave other lectures which the media communicated widely. I consider the ability to pursue this in peace and love a direct gift of God.

In the seminary we began to pray in a small group of six. We were awkward as we began to learn about praising God out loud, praying and singing in tongues, prophesying and using our emotions in a balanced way. We grew enough in a year to move our meeting to a

---

[1] Steve Clark is presently a leader of an ecumenical Christian community, *The Word of God,* in Ann Arbor, Michigan.

nearby convent and expand it to fifty people. The following year we were back in the seminary and numbering over a hundred.

Charismatic renewal became an issue in the life of the seminary. Many of the seminarians and Franciscan friars became involved in the renewal. Symposia discussions on charismatic renewal became a regular feature of seminary life. Most significantly, the presence of the renewal stimulated the prayer life throughout the seminary. I know of at least a dozen priest alumni who today lead charismatic renewal groups and prayer movements in their dioceses as a result of their involvement in the renewal in the seminary. During my years as Rector, I placed the highest priority on the formation of spiritual and pastoral leaders. Many men not equipped for leadership are sent to major seminaries. Many men who are students of theology and equipped in ministries of liturgy, catechetics or music, successfully complete the seminary program but are not prepared to form, lead, or pastor the people entrusted to them.

In the meantime, I was giving workshops on Penance and healing and was speaking at days of renewal around the country. In the summers I served as a consultant for houses of prayer and a speaker at contemplative workshops.

On Pentecost, 1974, I was walking in the hills, thanking God for his blessings and that he had called me to the beautiful life I had in Loretto. I particularly mentioned the recent overture of the Provincial whether I would be interested in being President of the College of Steubenville and that I was happy to have no ambition for that. I then heard deep in my spirit, the words: "What if I want you to be President?" I was stunned by this intervention of God and I stammered, "Well, if you want it, OK." Later, as I reflected on the incident, I put great weight on the word "if." God had said, *"if* I want you . . ." and I had replied, ". . . *if* you want it, OK." I went to a meeting of the search committee for a new president. I spoke of the changes needed in the College so that the spiritual identity of the College was given priority. The committee recommended my name only to the Board of Trustees. After additional discernment and on the condition that the Board accept my plan for revision of the College, I accepted the position and took office in July, 1974.

I accepted many speaking engagements that first year in order to alert the charismatic renewal to the new thrust at the College. In June of 1974, I had been in charge of the first major session proclaiming healing in the charismatic renewal. Francis MacNutt, O.P., Barbara Shlemon and Sister Briege McKenna were the main speakers but my involvement led me to be invited to teach on healing at the Regional Leaders Conferences on Charismatic Renewal. This in turn laid the basis for my being asked to lead the general session on the Vigil of Pentecost, 1975 in the Catacombs in Rome. I knew a fulfillment in that afternoon in Rome surpassed only by that evening in October 1969 when Jesus had baptized me in his Holy Spirit.

CHAPTER THREE

OTHER WITNESSES

In order for you, as a reader, to be able to identify with people who have had the same experience as I have, I have chosen people from a variety of backgrounds, ages and positions to witness to what God can do to change our lives. These are people whom I know, whose lives today are evidencing the love, commitment and service that will be powerful forces in renewing the Church.

Matthew Cramer

By the time I was 35, I had it made. My life was in order and the last thing I needed was Jesus. I had been raised a Catholic in a very religious family. I was faithful to my Church, attended Mass, received Communion regularly and supported the Church with my time and finances. My wife and I had been members of the choir, teachers and organizers of religious education programs, and had produced theatrical productions for the financial benefit of our parish. I was a commentator-lector at Sunday Liturgy. I believed in God, the sacraments, church tradition and authority. But it was belief, not experience.

Long ago I had rationalized that the world and its pleasures were there to be experienced and Church was for believing. If you believed and followed the rules, you could go to Heaven when you died. Religion could bring happiness, but only after you died. In the meantime, I was free to pursue the pleasures of the world as long as I didn't break any important rules. I had plenty of company. All of the people I knew were living in two worlds: Sunday and the rest of the week.

Of course there were conflicts between the laws of the world and the rules of the Church. But I learned quickly how to rationalize truth and handle my liquor. I had struck a fairly comfortable accommodation and was reasonably secure with my salary, position and possessions.

My wife had been pursuing a different approach. We were married very young (ages 19 and 17) and by this time had developed into entirely different people. She was experiencing peace, joy and a spiritual love I could not understand. Many times we would discuss our respective approaches. I could understand hers but I still felt mine was the right one. She would talk about spiritual experience but I could not, or would not, accept it as an option available for me.

Things finally reached a climax one weekend. My wife decided to get a group together and leave town to do maintenance work on a retreat house. I could see no purpose in going so I decided to stay home. I would be alone for a full week and free to do what I wanted. I could go out every night; my married man's dream was going to be fulfilled. I would be single again for a full week.

The first day I didn't do much. It was Sunday and I wanted to get things organized. Monday night, I got dinner over with early so I could start making the rounds. After dinner, I realized that Mondays weren't very good nights at the bars. There wasn't much action early in the week. I played music until 7 or 8, fixed myself a drink and turned on TV. TV lived up to its reputation and soon became boring. My last act was to belt down a couple of stiff drinks and go to bed.

I resolved in my hangover Tuesday morning to have fun that night. But after dinner, the same process repeated itself. I had everything I wanted, my house, my car, my stereo and color TV, and no restrictions on my nocturnal activities. But each time I thought of some fun thing to do, a later thought would show me how shallow it was. I began to see that the things I had wanted were not as rewarding as I had thought.

Tuesday melted away to Thursday and by Friday, I was near desperation. I had done nothing except consume $10 worth of alcohol which bought me a few hangovers. I began grasping at straws. What I needed was people. I needed someone to bum around with, laugh with and tell jokes to. But who? I had never cared enough for anyone to really establish a deep, lasting relationship. I knew several people who shared my sense of values, but they would only want to do the things I had already turned down all week.

Friday and Saturday nights are probably the best in the nocturnal circuit. But that didn't impress me. Even if I went out and did the fun things, I knew the happiness would not last and I would soon be right back where I started.

Saturday, my last day, was the most miserable day in my life. The morning was spent cleaning up the signs of my frustrating attempts to have fun. I was alone with my possessions, free to do what I wanted, but I was sad. Even the booze could not help. Stone cold sober, I sat down in my house to take stock of myself. What had happened? Why had I blown a full week and never done anything? Where was all the enjoyment I thought I would have? I had everything and yet, I had nothing.

Slowly, it began to dawn on me. I had been experiencing an object lesson. The pursuit of position, things and sensory experiences would reward me with emptiness. What I needed was something that could satisfy a deeper desire I had never recognized before. But what was it? What was my real need? And what could fill it?

My family would soon be coming home and I needed to get a grip on myself. I couldn't let them see how miserable I had been. But then, I felt a little joy. My family was coming home. They would bring me love. That was my real need. I needed love. I had been pursuing a need in an arena where there was no hope of filling it. I had learned how little return my desires brought me. There was no hope of ever being truly happy if I continued in my present direction.

The next several weeks were spent in quiet and sad reflection upon what I had learned. The message sank in until I was sure there would be no turning back. Each day while driving to and from work, I would try to think up some new direction to fill the void. Days turned into weeks with little results. There didn't seem to be any particular rush, just a steady desire to arrive at some conclusion.

After about three weeks, I had eliminated almost every possibility. The only thing I hadn't tried was what my wife was talking about, a personal experience of Christ. If it was true that you could experience Christ right here and now, that would be something. It would prove he really existed and maybe, give me some hope, but I was hesitant because those things were really weird. Sure, the saints were supposed to have had a communion with God, but I certainly wasn't one of them. My wife said she had experienced Christ many times, but there was no way I could believe it was really real.

Finally, I decided that I could return to my worldly pursuits somewhat wiser but bored and unhappy, or I could pursue this spiritual experience. It was risky, but I figured it wouldn't cost me much to at least pray and see what happened. If something happened, then I could explore it further. If nothing happened I could sadly return to the world. There was nothing to lose and maybe something to gain. So, one day on my way home from work, I said: "God, if there really is a personal experience of you, let me know it and I'll do what I can to respond."

Two weeks later, my wife asked a few people to come over and pray and she insisted that I attend. I had all but forgotten my prayer since nothing had happened. As the others began to pray, I sort of tuned them out and began to pray in myself about this "personal experience thing." I really wasn't praying hard, just trying to fill the time with something constructive.

What happened next is difficult to describe. In a very short space of time, but not with fearfulness, a tremendous peace descended upon me. It seemed to begin at the top of my head and quickly invaded my entire being. Then words began. The words were experienced, not heard. The words were for me and were somewhat critical of my past behavior but contained in those words were also total acceptance and an overwhelming love for me. I received the message without defensiveness because in the presence of such unbelievable love and acceptance I could be totally objective. The things I must do and the changes I must make were obvious and instantly I willed to do them.

Following that encounter, I had the firm conviction that I should attend the Life in the Spirit Seminars.[1] I had become convinced that somehow the training and reformation process I knew I needed to go through would begin there. Faithful to my part of the bargain, I went through the seminars at the next opportunity. I really didn't know what to expect. I learned about the gifts of the Spirit and began to understand that those gifts were to be part of my new relationship with God. My new life was to begin with accepting them and being trained in how to use them.

I was very interested to see what was in store for me after I was prayed with for the release of the Spirit. Having already encountered Jesus, I found it difficult to believe that more could be expected. But, shortly after, I received a hunger for scripture and I was able to understand it for the first time. It seemed to come alive. Communication with the Lord through scripture became regular. After three months, I could no longer praise him and return my love sufficiently in English. So I prayed for and received the gift of tongues. Significant changes in my way of living and working began to take place. I was now on my way to a whole new life. He truly had become for me the Way, the Truth and the Life.

Formerly a Manager of Administration and Fiscal Control at Aerojet Liquid Rocket Company, Sacramento, California, Matthew Cramer is now Head of Special Evangelism for the Servants of God's Love, a Catholic Covenant Community in Steubenville, Ohio.

[1] The Seminars are "designed to help people enter into a personal relationship with Christ, to yield to the action of the Holy Spirit, to become more deeply joined to a body of committed Christians and to grow in their relationship with Jesus Christ." New Covenant "News," March, 1979, p. 20.

Terri Rocco

When I was growing up, I always wanted to be a "good girl"; I always wanted to win the approval of my parents, teachers, God and the authority in my life—whatever situation I was in. I guess what I really wanted was acceptance and love.

As I recall my life, I always felt very deeply about things; I was very sensitive to feeling loved or feeling hurt. I remember that just a mean look from my grandfather or my father could send me into tears and sadness. In high school I was hurt through several different situations: an ended love relationship, the peer pressure of keeping up with my richer friends, being popular, looking right, dressing right, knowing the right people and being seen with them, generally having to earn love and acceptance again.

By college there was a rebellion and anger in me. I was tired of trying to somehow be what others wanted me to be. Some of it was caused by the unrest of the '60s, I'm sure. Nevertheless, I wanted to fight back at something—my parents, my background, my "good girl" efforts. My dress code regressed to blue jeans and a flannel shirt for *all* occasions. I generally said to everyone who meant something to me; "I don't care if I'm a good girl, I don't care if I have your approval. What do *I* want to do? What do *I* want to be?" I searched for self-identity through many things in my freshmen and sophomore years. I drank every chance I could; I felt like the rebel and I loved it. I joined a sorority to have fun and party and secondly, to have a popular position on campus.

In my sophomore year I became involved with some drugs. I liked the feeling of being "high" and being removed from the ordinary, boring world of life. I was funny when I was "high." People laughed and enjoyed my humor. I was loved and somehow I was saying: "I don't need to be GOOD."

It's ironic that during my times alone, being high on hash or grass, that I'd think. I'd think very deeply about life and my reasons for living. I became thoughtful when high and began writing my questions and mental wonderings on paper. The Lord was working even then to stir up the right questions in me.

That following semester I took a required theology course entitled "Christian Moral Principles." The instructor was raising the same questions in class that seemed to be raised in me during those times of searching. Somehow, he seemed to have some answers. That was the beginning of turning my life to Jesus. Slowly, from deep within me, something wanted to know that there was a purpose for my life, for my hurt and pain. I really hoped that this priest was telling the truth. I wanted him to give some reasons for living and "being good" and being responsible.

Through a series of situations I found myself at a point where I was sitting with a fellow student in my dorm room. She had a New Testament and asked if she could pray. I agreed. As she prayed out loud and spoke with God as if he were sitting right there, I began to feel a warmth move through my "insides." I felt a presence of love that brought tears to my eyes. I knew I had experienced God—the way I remembered when I'd come back to my pew after communion back in the third grade. I wanted to pray to God, too. That quickly, I began to pray. I asked him to please stay close to me. I told him how it was to live by myself and to try to solve life's problems by myself.

Gradually, through theology classes, prayer meetings and some fellowship, I began to grow. I wanted to be "good" and upright but somehow it was different. The gift of tongues, gift of prophecy and interpretation, a strong faith and hope, a sense of really being happy and filled with joy were mine. It all seemed to be happening so fast. I came on fire with a life that has never left me.

Eight years ago when I received the fullness of the Holy Spirit, I was sure there could be no more to receive. I must have been given it all. But there was so much more I couldn't then comprehend. Today the reality of Jesus is my purpose for living. He has indeed become my portion and my cup. Everything flows from him and his word.

My friendships are no longer based or dependent on popularity or outdoing one another; they are based on my commitment to love my brothers and sisters. I understand now that my ability to receive love and to give it flows from my identity as a daughter of the Lord of Lords.

The way I dress needs to simply be an outward expression of my delight in being a woman of God who is growing day by day in a delight of her womanhood. No longer do my clothes need to be a symbol of rebellion or of "peer pressure." My goodness is not flowing from a need in me to somehow win the love and affection of others but somehow through God's grace and strength I desire to be good and to do good for others. I suppose as I am formed into his likeness I begin to take on the characteristics of my Lord.

The fight for popularity is almost gone. I know now that I have a place in the family of God and it is not necessary to look prettier or dress sharper or have a more handsome boyfriend than someone else. There is a deep peace within my spirit that gives me the awareness that God walks with me.

In him you too were chosen; when you heard the glad tidings of salvation, the word of truth and believed in it, you were sealed with the Holy Spirit who had been promised. He is the pledge of our inheritance, the first payment against the full redemption of a people God has made his own, to praise his glory.   Ephesians 1:13–14.

A graduate of the College of Steubenville, Terri Rocco is now an administrative assistant in the community office of the Servants of God's Love and is in a position of pastoral leadership for a group of single women in that community.

Terry Flanagan

As a wife and mother committed to developing Christian family life, I so often reflect on my early attempts to know the Lord and of his great mercy to me.

The first time I experienced Jesus I was in the first grade. The Sister who prepared me for my First Holy Communion gave me such a love for Jesus that I decided I wanted to marry him when I got big. In my first grade understanding that meant I should become a nun.

As I was growing up, my love for Jesus came and went until high school where I again came into an experience of the living Lord. I was a senior in high school. Because of a shortage of lockers I had to share mine with another girl. I noticed she kept small bags of marijuana in the locker. Later in the year things were different about her. The marijuana was gone and she spoke of a club called Young Life of which she was now a member. She also spoke of a person she called J.C. who had changed her life. Later she told me his real name was Jesus Christ. Since I was a Catholic, my parents wouldn't let me go to Young Life until one day I heard that the priest from our parish had spoken at a meeting. My parents agreed to let me go. I went for the rest of my senior year and there came to know Jesus as my friend, someone who would be with me no matter what. Whenever I needed him, he'd be there. In my fervor, I decided to read the Bible but, after finishing Genesis, I gave up because I just didn't "get anything out of it."

The next fall I went to college in Erie, Pa. When I left home I left all my friends, including Jesus, behind. By my sophomore year I had gone from a shy, religious type girl to a rather wild one. I got into excessive drinking and smoking, unwholesome relationships with guys and into drugs. I hated myself and the things I did. But the more I hated myself, the deeper I seemed to get until I wanted to find a hole, crawl into it and never come out again. God had better plans.

During the second semester of my sophomore year, there was an overnighter. A couple who had been on drugs were to share the dangers of drugs and there were to be some informative films. A group of us decided to go just to get out of the dorm for the night. That evening after the talks and films as we sat around talking, I noticed a girl sitting by herself. I went over to see if I could help. At that time she said, "No," but later she returned to ask if I would help her. She was on drugs and was trying to avoid the temptation of taking a downer to go to sleep. Around three in the morning we went to a little chapel to talk since she still couldn't sleep. I told her about the girl in high school who kept marijuana in her locker. I told her how different this girl was once she met Jesus. That night was the changing point of my life. I agreed to go to a prayer meeting with her for I knew it was what she needed. Little did I know it was what I needed too. That night when I went into the prayer meeting, I knew a presence of God there that I remembered from Young Life meetings. That night for the first time I met Jesus as my savior. I experienced all my sins being washed away. I felt new. I could start again.

After the prayer meeting, when I was going to sleep, a song we had sung came back to me: "No Turning Back." I knew I needed to make a decision to either give my life to Jesus and not go back to the old life style or to continue as I had. I gave my life that night to Jesus and in return he has given me the happiest, fullest life I could have ever wanted.

The following week I started a Life in the Spirit series. Those seven weeks of the series were like a dream to me. Those around me noticed the change. Even my college basketball coach pulled me aside one day to ask me why I was so happy. She had never seen me so happy.

Since that night when I received the Baptism in the Spirit, my love for God's word has grown and so has my understanding. I have the power to live the life I wasn't able to live before. I have the freedom to be me—free from the many fears and insecurities that I had before. Some of the changes that have happened in me have come slowly. Others have come just by being loved by his people.

Terry Flanagan is the wife of Jack Flanagan, the mother of one and a half year old Michelle. She shares in the responsibility for the care and support of married women in the Servants of God's Love.

Tony Corasaniti

I think basically I've always been a person striving to be good. I was raised by good parents. I had a mother who was a very faithful Catholic and a model of faith for me. I always appreciated the Church life I had come to know from my earliest years. When some of my friends in high school stopped going to church, I still went, not only out of duty but also out of desire. I had some exposure to drugs in high school but only because it was the thing to do and so I did it.

During my last two years in high school, I became very depressed on the inside while still showing the exterior of a "good guy." I think I was depressed because I could not find meaning for the things I was doing. I searched a lot but never seemed to find what I was looking for in my life. I wanted to leave my family, my friends, my city. All I was searching for was to be happy and to share that happiness with others. For me, God was a part of what I looked for because I believed in him, although I did not know him. My senior year in high school I came in touch with him on a youth retreat weekend. I knew an experience of his love that weekend which let me know he was indeed part of what I was searching for in my life. Only then I did not know he was ALL I was looking for, so I did not really commit my life to him. This was also the response of many of my friends who had made the retreat. As a result, the experience I had gradually wore off and I found myself back where I started.

My first year at college I remained in the city and commuted back and forth from school. Being in my home town made me even more depressed. I did more things, just for kicks to try and make my life seem better but it never worked. I was still unhappy. I saw myself as a person who had a good heart and good intentions but whose life seemed to lack something essential. My one big dream was to move away and start my life over again. For me, this meant happiness and a better life.

At the beginning of the spring semester of my first year at college, the Lord moved in my life with the purpose of giving me a new one. In the course of four short days, I came to know Jesus personally in a way I had never known before. I heard someone mention the Baptism in the Spirit on a Thursday evening and by Sunday I was asking people to pray with me for the fullness of the Spirit to be released in my life. During the course of those four days I experienced the Lord working directly in my life. I attended a Full Gospel Businessmen's meeting at which Father Michael Scanlan, the President of the College, gave his testimony of how the Lord had worked in his life. As I heard people praising the Lord in various ways I joined in with them all the while saying to the friends who had brought me: "You'll have to explain this to me afterwards." During my sleep that night I was awakened three times hearing a knock at my bedroom door and my name being called each time. The last time I began to praise the Lord aloud because I believed he was waking me for that purpose. I believed I was baptized in the Spirit that night but on that following Sunday, I spoke with Father Michael about what had been happening over the weekend and he prayed with me for the release of the Spirit.

Since that time my life has changed. Where I was once a good-intentioned person, I am a better man now because I know him. The Christian life I had once just appreciated as a young boy, I now cherish and commit myself to as a man. I now have the life I've always wanted, the life I've always looked for, the life that was really mine from the beginning.

Anthony Corasaniti, a graduate of the College of Steubenville, works full-time in ministry to the poor in the Diocese of Steubenville. He also serves in pastoral care for a group of single men in the Servant of God's Love community.

Sister Ann Shields

At the time I was prayed with for the full release of the Spirit in my life, I had been a Sister of Mercy for thirteen years. While life had had some substantial difficulty at one point, basically I was satisfied as a religious and as a successful high school teacher. Still, there was a pervasive emptiness. Through the invitation of an elderly sister in the convent where I lived, I had attended the first two prayer meetings of the only prayer group then in the Diocese of Altoona-Johnstown (PA). While I appreciated much that was prayed and taught, my cautious nature held me back from looking too closely or exploring too deeply.

But, on a cold, wintry Saturday morning following the second prayer meeting, I awoke with a deeper emptiness than ever before. In response to it I decided to visit a cloistered Carmelite sister, some twenty miles away who was a good friend of many years. That afternoon Sister Robin Stratton, OCD, and I prayed for over two hours. At the end of that time she simply said to me: "Betsey, what do you want?" I replied: "You know, I've made vows, committed my life to Jesus Christ but I still believe I'm going my own way. I just want to surrender my life as I've never done before." We prayed. Minutes later, my ride home was announced and I left. The hours that followed were busy ones and left me no time for reflection. I had had no emotional experience; still I knew I had made a major decision.

The following afternoon, returning from several hours of directing a high school play, I trudged wearily into the convent chapel. "Lord," I prayed, "you know how weak I am; if you heard my prayer yesterday and you desire to possess my life more fully, please let me know your presence."

My mind then clicked into the work at hand. I left the chapel to "begin" the never-ending task of correcting essays and themes and book reports.

Suddenly, in the middle of the hall leading to my room, I was literally invaded by joy. I stopped, letting it permeate my body, mind and spirit. While I relished it, I could not let myself believe this was the answer to my prayer. Surely it will go, I thought. It did not. Surely, after dinner and meetings, it will go. It did not. Surely, by tomorrow morning it will be gone. It was not. In eight years it has never gone. Sometimes it wells up to overflowing; often it is quiet and simple and deep—but it never goes.

The joy of the Lord, as the Psalmist says, has become my strength. The emptiness has never returned. I did not have to look to a new career, more graduate study, undertaking more duties at school or in my community to fill my emptiness. The Lord himself has become my life.

Caution again held me back from yielding to the gift of tongues. I wasn't sure about its authenticity—I felt foolish—I didn't want to be caught up in anything more risky than I already was. Three months after the initial prayer with my friend, Robin, at Carmel I knelt late one night in our convent chapel. No one was home so I was praying aloud in gratitude "for he who is mighty had done great things for me." As I prayed, I remember telling the Lord my heart so overflowed I had no words any longer to express my gratefulness. As soon as these words were out of my mouth, they were followed by odd syllables—immediately, I stopped—then prayed again and again the odd syllables came forth. I could control it; I could stop it but I reflected: this must be the gift of tongues. I've trusted the Lord this far . . . so I relaxed and rising up in me came a spirit of praise and prayer I had never experienced before. I didn't reflect on it again that evening—just allowed it to be.

Soon it dawned on me that this experience of joy, this new language of praise was a manifestation of the Spirit of God in *me*. I understood for the first time what it meant to be a temple of the Holy Spirit. The Spirit was using me to praise his Father because I allowed him. Every time I prayed in tongues, I was tapping into the praise of the Spirit constantly being given to the Father. My caution flew to the winds and I submitted to the work of God in me.

Today, eight years later, God's work in me continues. The baptism in the Spirit was but the beginning of new life in Jesus Christ. Daily I learn what it is to die and rise with him: to submit to his will, to lay down my life for his Church—the People of God here in Steubenville.

Whatever lies ahead for me, I know now a faithful God in whom I can put my trust—for I have come to know the fullness of life that can be found only in Jesus Christ.

Sister Ann Shields, RSM, is a member of the National Service Committee for Catholic Charismatic Renewal in the United States. She serves the community in Steubenville through pastoral care for the Christian formation of women.

. . .

Sometimes, when we hear someone reflect on his or her life as these men and women have just done, there is a tendency to say either:

"That's all right for him or her but it's not for me. My personality is different. God deals with me much differently."

or

If we depend on emotional experience for our spiritual life, we're in for a downfall. That's been one of the great assets of the Catholic Church—that it bases our growth in the Christian life on the teaching of the Church from Scripture and tradition and the sacramental life. Experience comes and goes; we can be too easily deceived. It seems as though the renewal is based on experience and that's too risky. It's not for me."

There's some truth in both these views. But the people who have given these testimonies would respond: While we experience the same concerns which you do, nevertheless, we testify to a substantial and more permanent difference in our lives based on the experience of the power of God; a difference which flows from knowing the Lord, not just knowing about him; from living in the power of the Holy Spirit, not just believing in the Holy Spirit. For these reasons, I believe we need to reflect on the teaching of the Catholic Church regarding the Trinity, the life of the Holy Spirit within us and his gifts.

CHAPTER FOUR

THE HOLY SPIRIT

The Holy Spirit has variously been called the unknown, overlooked or mystery person of the Holy Trinity. Catholics pray frequently to Our Father and my
Father. They pray easily to Jesus Christ, the Redeemer
and King. But, with the exception of the hymn, "Come
Holy Ghost" and the invocation prayer "Come, Holy
Spirit," they seldom attest to the Third Person of the
Family of God and when they do, it is not in the same
"real person" way that they refer to the Father and Son.

The charismatic renewal has emphasized the reality
and immediacy of the Holy Spirit. It has embraced the
truth of the equality of the Holy Spirit as a person equal
to the Father and Son. The renewal has brought this
emphasis to the Holy Spirit, not just in proclamation
and teaching but in experience. The experience of the
Holy Spirit is so immediate and powerful that it evokes
a natural response of praise for this person in the Family
of God.

Only when the Holy Spirit is given an equal place
with the Father and Son does the Family of God become
a reality for us. The family is trinitarian and it is the
Holy Spirit who is the life and love, the binding force of

the family. When we are living in the Spirit we are caught up in God's family. When we do not live in the Spirit, we cannot be living the intended life of God's family.

In the last chapter I explained how, following the release of the Spirit, I was caught up in the prayer of the family of God. I also explained that suddenly the Spirit in me was able to be contacted by the Spirit in the inspired Word of God with the result that all scripture had new power and new meaning for me. I found myself and my participation in God's life there in the written words of the Bible.

In this chapter, I am going to express what it means to live in the Family of God in the power of the Holy Spirit. I am also going to show from scripture passages the importance of the Holy Spirit in the life of Jesus, the lives of the disciples and therefore also in our lives. I will quote the key passages which gave me insight and strength in this area. Before I experienced the release of the Holy Spirit, these passages had much less meaning for me; indeed they seemed less important and helpful than many other sections of the New Testament. Since the release of the Spirit, I have found the truth of the words John quotes Jesus using to Nicodemus:

> Jesus answered him, "Truly, truly, I say to you, unless one is born anew, he cannot see the kingdom of God. Nicodemus said to him, "How can a man be born when he is old? Can he enter a second time into his mother's womb and be born?" Jesus answered, "Truly, truly, I say to you, unless one is born of water and the spirit, he cannot enter the kingdom of God." (John 3:5)

This, then, is how we are to see the Holy Spirit in the family of God.

God is a family of total love, total commitment, total self giving. The Father so loves the Son that he gives his total self to the Son, does all things through him and places all creation under his domain. The Son so loves the Father that he does nothing of himself but does only what he hears from the Father and acts only for the glory of the Father and not for his own glory. (Phil. 2) This mutual total gift binds the Father and Son together in that love, that force, that power which we call the Holy Spirit. Both Father and Son are so totally expressed in this love that the love itself is a person, a member of the Family of God. Indeed, the Holy Spirit is Lord just as the Father is Lord and the Son is Lord.

The family of God invites all men and women to join the family and to enter into the inner life of the family. The invitation comes forth to each person: "Join us and live our life forever. Come and take the Father as your father, be an adopted son or daughter. Come take Jesus the only begotten son as your savior, redeemer, Lord and brother. Come take the Holy Spirit as the Spirit, the power, the love and the binding force in your life. (Eph. 4) Come enter into the Family of God. Enter into the Father's delight in his Son, the Son's praise and glorifying of the Father and the Spirit of love which alone can effect total unity."

To enter into the family of God it is necessary to enter into a new relationship with each person: Father, Son and Spirit. There are to be intimate bonds of relationships with each and this can happen only through a process of conversion and committment. We are each called to turn from any and all whom we would treat as our ultimate father and to proclaim that we have but one Father, the Creator of heaven and earth and he alone is sufficient for all our needs so that we can trust him as loving father, intimate caring father, abba.

We are called to turn from anything and any person whom we would see or treat as Lord, as the one rightly directing our lives. Most of all, we are called to turn from ourselves, give up our assertions and patterns of seeking to direct our own lives and be captains and master of our own soul. We are called to take Jesus as Lord and Master, captain and teacher. He is to be placed in the center of all we are and all we do. He will reign as King of Kings and Lord of Lords. He will direct our lives for our own best good, for extending the reign of God and for the glory of the Father. He will lead us to serve others as he served, to love others as he loved, to complete in the circumstances of our lives what remains to be done so that the suffering of Jesus Christ will bring forth their intended results.

Finally, we are called to open our lives to the full living power of the Holy Spirit. We are called to turn from seeking guidance, strength, consolation and power to love from any source contrary to the workings of the Holy Spirit. In the Spirit alone can we have the foundation to integrate and direct all things in our lives. In the Spirit alone can we trust ourselves to total loving and total giving. Without the Holy Spirit we cannot proclaim the Lordship of Jesus, we cannot give pure worship to the Father, we cannot love selflessly with what the gospels call agape love, we cannot bring forth lasting fruit and we will not see the fruits of love, joy, peace, patience, kindness and long suffering in our lives.

We are the ones who must make the explicit choices of God the Father, God the Son and God the Spirit. We choose the proper relationship with each and to the extent that we convert and commit ourselves to this living in the Family of God, we are received into the relationships, we receive the life, power and graces to sustain us and we know in an experiential way the truth of our life with God.

The New Testament presents a very special series of events by which Jesus, the Apostles and Christians in general, enter into an intimate relationship with the Holy Spirit. Most people are startled to discover the transforming relationship between Jesus and the Holy Spirit. St. Luke presents a clear description of the progress of this relationship, first, between Jesus and the Spirit during his lifetime and then, between the Body of Jesus or the Church and the Spirit after his death, resurrection and ascension.

First, we should note that the name "Christ" means "anointed by the Spirit." The angel replies to Mary's question about the birth of Jesus, saying "The Holy Spirit will come upon you and the power of the Most High will overshadow you." (Luke 1:35) Luke does not present the Spirit as actively working in the life of Jesus until his thirtieth year when John baptizes him in the Jordan.

> When all the people were baptized and Jesus was at prayer after likewise being baptized, the skies opened and the Holy Spirit descended on him in visible form like a dove. A voice from heaven was heard to say "You are my beloved son. On you my favor rests." (Luke 3:21–22)

From that time on Luke presents Jesus as directed and empowered by the Spirit.

> Jesus, full of the Holy Spirit, then returned from the Jordan and was conducted by the Spirit into the desert. (Luke 4:1)
>
> Jesus returned in the power of the Spirit to Galilee and his reputation spread throughout the region (Luke 4:14)
>
> When the book of the prophet Isaiah was handed him, he unrolled the scroll and found the passage where it was written, "The Spirit of the Lord is within me, therefore he has anointed me. (Luke 4:17–18)

They were spellbound by his teaching for his words had authority. (Luke 4:32)

He commands the unclean spirits with authority and power and they leave. (Luke 4:36)

One day Jesus was teaching and the power of the Lord made him heal. (Luke 5:17)

It is clear from the above passages that Luke is teaching us that the descent of the Holy Spirit empowered Jesus into his public mission. Luke is teaching that this empowering was the primary impetus of his works, though it is related to the divine nature of Jesus by which he was the only Son of the Father. This nature certainly established the basic relationship by which Jesus was Savior and Redeemer, but Luke ascribes the directing of Jesus' life to the Holy Spirit given to him at the Jordan.

It seems correct to conclude that Luke is emphasizing this point so that Christians will acknowledge the empowering of their lives as coming from the same Holy Spirit now given on Pentecost and at subsequent occasions flowing from the Pentecost event.

Luke makes this point clear in his treatment of the empowering of the Apostolic Church in the Acts of the Apostles. He describes the initial Pentecost experience: "All were filled with the Holy Spirit. They began to express themselves in foreign tongues and make bold proclamations as the Spirit prompted them." (Acts 2:4)

He relates Peter's explanation of the event in terms of a pouring out of the Spirit:

No, it is what Joel the prophet spoke of: It shall come to pass in the last days, says God, that I will pour out a portion of my spirit on all mankind. Your sons and daughters shall prophesy, your young men shall see visions and your old men shall dream dreams. Yes, even on my servants and handmaids I will pour out a portion of my spirit in those days. (Acts 2:16–17)

Peter later states: "Exalted at God's right hand he first received the promised Holy Spirit from the Father, then poured the Spirit out on us. This is what you now see and hear. (Acts 2:33)

Just as the outpouring of the Spirit on Jesus led to his healing others in the subsequent chapter, so the outpouring of the Spirit on the Church in Acts 2 leads to Peter healing the lame man in Acts 3: "Then Peter said 'I have neither silver nor gold but what I have I give you! In the name of Jesus Christ the Nazarean, walk.' " (Acts 3:6)

As Jesus is tested by Satan after the Spirit leads him into the desert, so Peter is tested by the elders and scribes in Jerusalem. Luke describes Peter's response to the question, "By what power or in whose name have men of your stripe done this?" Then, Peter filled with the Holy Spirit, spoke up. (Acts 4:7–8)

Peter now exhibits the same otherness of overwhelming authority that marked Jesus' teaching following his baptism at the Jordan.

This falling of the Holy Spirit is proclaimed by Luke not as a one time Pentecost experience but as an ongoing event in the life of the Christian Church: "The place where they were gathered shook as they prayed. They were filled with the Holy Spirit and continued to speak God's word with confidence." (Acts 4:31)

Peter's rebuke to Ananias and Sapphira is based on their attempting to deceive the Holy Spirit who directs the life of the Christian community: "How could you two scheme to put the Spirit of the Lord to the test?" (Acts 5:9)

Stephen, who will be the first martyr, is selected to be a deacon and described as "a man filled with faith and the Holy Spirit." (Acts 6:5) He then accused his persecutors: . . ". . You are always opposing the Holy Spirit just as your fathers did before you." (Acts 7:51) While Luke describes him: "Stephen meanwhile filled with the Holy Spirit looked to the sky above and saw the glory of God and Jesus standing at God's right hand." (Acts 7:55) Stephen at the end prays: "Lord Jesus, receive my spirit." He fell to his knees and cried out in a loud voice, "Lord, do not hold this sin against them." And with that he died. (Acts 7:59–60)

Luke is drawing an obvious parallel to the death of Jesus. "Jesus uttered a loud cry and said, 'Father, into your hands I recommend my spirit.' After he said this, he expired." (Luke 23:46) "Jesus said 'Father, forgive them, they do not know what they are doing.'" (Luke 23:34)

Luke is teaching us that we are to follow the same path of life, led by the same Spirit to accomplish the same works as Jesus did. Philip is thus directed by the Spirit to the eunuch and when the work is completed the Spirit snatches Philip away. (Acts 9:29–40)

The outpouring of the Holy Spirit is not confined to one time or one place. Peter and John impose hands on the Samaritan converts and "they received the Holy Spirit." (Acts 8:18) This is a discernible transformation by the power of the Spirit as is evident by Simon the Magician's offer to buy the power "so that if I place my hands on anyone he will receive the Holy Spirit." (Acts 8:19)

Ananias comes to Saul in order that he be healed and "be filled with the Holy Spirit." (Acts 8:47)

The Gentiles likewise receive the Spirit as the Jews did on Pentecost:

Peter had not finished these words when the Holy Spirit descended upon all who were listening to Peter's message. The circumcised believers who had accompanied Peter were surprised that the gift of the Holy Spirit should have been poured out on the Gentiles also, whom they could hear speaking in tongues and glorifying God. Peter put the question at this point, "What can stop these people who have received the Holy Spirit even as we have from being baptized with water?" (Acts 10:44–47)

The missionary work of Paul is described as empowered and directed by the Holy Spirit.

On one occasion while they were engaged in the Liturgy of the Lord and were fasting, the Holy Spirit spoke to them. "Set apart Barnabas and Saul for me to do the work for which I have called them." (Acts 13:2) . . . . These two sent forth by the Holy Spirit went down to the Port of Seleucia and set sail from there for Cyprus. (Acts 13:4)

Luke frequently refers to the empowering and directing force of the Holy Spirit in Paul's missionary activities: Acts 13:9, Acts 13:52, Acts 16:7. In Ephesus, Paul, as Peter and John had done earlier, lays hands on the converts and the Holy Spirit comes on them. "As Paul laid his hands on them the Holy Spirit came down on them and they began to speak in tongues and to utter prophecies." (Acts 19:6)

In the early church a new convert seeking life in God's family was received into the Christian Community, the Church, through the rites of Baptism, Confirmation and Eucharist. In Baptism the Church emphasized that the convert was now a child of the Father belonging to the Lord Jesus Christ and signed and sealed forever with a new character. In Confirmation the Church proclaimed that the convert was set aside and empowered as a witness of the Kingdom and a soldier in God's army for the full reign of the Kingdom of God. In Eucharist the Church proclaimed that the convert was a member of the worshipping community, one who was joined with Christ in his death and resurrection, one who lives as a member of his Body and was nurtured in his Body and Blood. These sacraments were intended to bring to the recipient the fullest participation in the life of the family of God that was possible for him or her to receive at that time. As infant baptism became more common in the Church, the infants entered into the new relationship but were not capable of making the commitments and appropriating into their lives the graces available. In order to give more meaning to the sacraments and to enable the recipients to appropriate and come alive to what is transpiring, Confirmation and Eucharist were separated from Baptism and conferred in later years. This certainly enabled people to appreciate the gift of these sacraments and to prepare to enter a new level of spiritual life through them.

What millions of Catholics have discovered in the past twelve years is that they can enter into a deeper level of life in the family of God and know a new empowering in the Holy Spirit, through making an act of total commitment to the Lord and inviting the Holy Spirit to take over their lives. This action is what is meant by "being baptized in the Holy Spirit" or by "receiving the release of the Holy Spirit." In one sense, this is not a new dimension of God's life since it is exactly the intention of the sacraments of Baptism, Confirmation and Eucharist. But, in another sense, it is distinctly empowering and for the great majority of people the most intimate, powerful and transforming spiritual experience in their lives to that point. The result of being baptized in the Spirit is to know a new fullness in the relationship of the Family of God and, most clearly, to know the empowering of the Holy Spirit to live those relationships.

The result of being baptized in the Spirit has ongoing and deepening ramifications. Though I was baptized in the Spirit years ago, I recently realized that my prayer, my vocation as a Franciscan and priest, my ministry in preaching, teaching and bringing healing to the Body of Christ was based on a faith still lacking in a certain intimacy. This realization came about through caring for my stepfather during a long term illness immediately preceding his death. The days I spent near him I would pray, celebrate Mass, seek the Lord on how I should care that day for my stepfather but always I would leave the hospital with a spiritual heaviness, a sadness and a physical weariness I could not seem to break through. Over the months I sought God on how to deal with this problem but there seemed to be no answer. Then one day not long before my stepfather's death, a new clarity on how the Lord wanted to relate to me and me to him came into my life. I realized that while I believed God loved me, I didn't have faith to live in the relationships of God's family. I believed in God's free gift of salvation, his presence in my life, the guidance and strengthening of the Holy Spirit and that I was an heir of the kingdom, one who would live forever. I believed all this and I based my life on this, but I wasn't living the life of God's family. I called God Father, Abba, in prayer and believed he was my Father but I didn't relate to him as Jesus did. I wasn't going to him for all things and expecting the strength of my relationship as son to be the recreating force of my life. I wasn't resting and basking in my sonship so that I could be more of a son as I went back to his people.

I also wasn't relating to Jesus as my brother who was also my Savior, Redeemer, Rescuer and Lord. I was relating to him as Lord, Savior, Redeemer and Rescuer but this alone did not put me into the conscious life of God's family. I could be the saved one, the rescued one and the redeemed one and still be on the outside of the immediate family. I could relate to Jesus as Lord and still be part of the kingdom, part of the army or one of the servants of the Lord. But when I related to him as my brother who was also all of this, then I was consciously inserted in the life of the family. As redeemed, rescued and saved, I could thank him, as under his lordship, I could bow before him and maybe, clutch at his feet. But as brother I could cling to him, I could embrace him, I could discover my place as the beloved disciple who could rest his head on the chest of the master. Suddenly, the meaning of John's Gospel came alive. John wasn't just speaking of himself when he wrote of "the disciple whom Jesus loved" (John 13:23) or the disciple who leaned his head on the breast of Jesus (John 13:25). He was referring to all who would love Jesus as an elder brother, all who would seek intimacy with him and trust him with affectionate love. He was calling me to be that beloved and to move into my relationship with Jesus in the family of God.

Finally, I wasn't relating to the Spirit as Lord and third person of the trinitarian family of God. I discovered that relating to the Spirit means inserting myself into the intimate power, the life of love in the Family. It means being caught up in relating to the Father and the Son Jesus that I am inserted in the powerful love dynamic of the relationship, so inserted in it that I am identified with the Person of the Holy Spirit. I found that the more I related to the Father as son and the Son as brother then I, spontaneously, did what I had striven to do for so long . . . I praised Father and Son, I worshipped the Father and Son, I adored the Father and Son. I dwelt in the presence of the Father and Son as a person fully present and involved.

For years I had known the power of praise. I knew when I praised God, I was lifted beyond my circumstances. I knew that when I praised God I received a new perspective on life and I knew at times that my praising God had been a channel for his grace and healing power. Situations had been changed and people had been healed because I had been a willing channel of praise. But even through those wonderful times, I knew something was lacking. I knew I was deciding to praise and leaping to praise. I knew I was exerting great energy to sustain praise. It was good but not enough. I knew deep down that praise like love should be the result of the relationship. It should flow from something more basic.

Suddenly it was clear that as I claimed my place in the Family of God, as I took my place as son to the Father and brother (redeemed and saved) to my brother and Lord, what happened in me naturally and spontaneously what flowed out of me because of where I was and how I was relating was praise. I praised my beautiful, powerful and loving Father. I praised my strong, loving, self-sacrificing, all-knowing brother, my Lord Jesus. I praised because I was looking at them from the right position, I was believing in them from the intimate stance of a member of the family. This praise was a family matter. It was the way the family of God related. I knew the Holy Spirit as Lord because this relationship, this praise and thanks was an overwhelming reality of presence. It wasn't the Father or the Son, it was the relationship between them. It was the bond of life and love between them. It was the power flowing through me to be caught up in their love affair. It was being in the main stream of true, eternal life. It was being in the center of the river of life. It had power and fruitfulness. I was able to seek guidance in that relationship and river of life, and care for my stepfather with new freedom and peace.

This experience of being baptized in the Holy Spirit is not confined to those involved in today's charismatic renewal. The lives of the saints frequently contain accounts of such an experience. St. Symeon, the New Theologian, wrote extensively of this experience in the tenth century. The accounts of St. Francis of Assisi and many founders of new orders and renewal movements contain similar references. I know of men and women who have experienced this release of the Spirit through the commitments they have made in Cursillo, Marriage Encounter and similar renewal programs. Nevertheless, the overwhelming number of Catholics who have received this release of the Spirit have done so through charismatic renewal. This experience is the main foundation or hallmark of the charismatic renewal. Following this release, people begin to experience and minister with new spiritual gifts. They praise God in the new manner of praying in tongues, they experience distinct movements of grace, giving them words of knowledge, words of wisdom or prophecy. They may receive a healing or pray for another person who is then healed. They know a new dimension of their spiritual life, one of living with special graces or gifts called charisms. Thus, they say they are involved in the charismatic renewal of the Church.

For so much of our Catholic lives we have made decisions based on faith and doctrine to pattern our lives according to Jesus Christ, and while laudable, it has often resulted in will-power Christianity. Such an approach to life in the kingdom of God can drain us of the vitality and riches of the Good News. It is true that we are called as a Christian people to face difficulty and the sufferings of life with firmness, consistency and stability born of faith and a disciplined will but it is equally true that God wants us to know and experience here in our earthly life what Paul calls the "first pledge of our inheritance"—the Spirit of God. It is this life of the Spirit fully activated within us that makes it possible to live the Gospel as it was intended—with joy and power.

In the power of the Spirit, then, we need to rediscover the gifts of the Spirit, the gifts enumerated in Paul's first letter to the Corinthians, chapter twelve. These are the tools God gives us to hear his voice and live a full Christian life. They are not based on our worthiness or our holiness. They are given to us that we might become the holy people of God—that we might know our inheritance having been baptized into his life.

Now concerning spiritual gifts, brethren, I do not want you to be uninformed. . . . Now there are varieties of gifts but the same Spirit; and there are varieties of service but the same Lord; and there are varieties of working, but it is the same God who inspires them all in everyone. To each is given the manifestation of the Spirit for the common good. To one is given through the Spirit the utterance of wisdom, and to another the utterance of knowledge according to the same Spirit, to another faith by the same Spirit, to another gifts of healing by the one Spirit, to another the working of miracles, to another prophecy, to another the ability to distinguish between spirits, to another various kinds of tongues, to another the interpretation of tongues. All these are inspired by one and the same Spirit, who apportions to each one individually as he wills. 1 Corinthians 12:1, 4–11

I want to say some things about spiritual gifts as Paul writes of them in this well-known passage. Paul tells the

Church at Corinth that he wants them to be knowledge-able concerning the gifts of the Spirit—that everything they are experiencing comes as a gracious gift of God's Spirit. He wants them to understand all the gifts of God so that they (the Corinthians) would be able to acknowl-edge the Lord as the source of all blessings. He wants to teach them in chapters twelve to fourteen how these gifts are to function because Paul is well aware that, while the gifts are meant to be sources of strength and wisdom for God's people, they can easily be occasions of difficulty when not used in accord with the will of God.

Too often today we hear that the gifts were intended for the early church to "get it started." Yet, no where in Paul's writings do we find even a hint that spiritual gifts were intended to be temporary.

St. Thomas Aquinas, in his *Summa Theologica* in the section called "Graces freely given," taught that God's people need special gifts to understand the truths of faith because they are beyond human power to know—to know in a way that such truths can then be preached.[1]

In contemporary history, the council fathers in their Decree on the Lay Apostolate, Section 3, state:

For the exercise of this apostolate, the Holy Spirit who sanctifies the people of God through the ministry and the sacraments, gives to the faithful special gifts as well (cf., 1 Cor. 12:7) "alloting to everyone according as he wills" (1 Cor. 12:11). Thus, may the individual according' to the gifts that each has received, administer it to one another and become "good stewards of the manifold grace of God," (1 Pt. 4:10) and build up the whole body in charity (cf. Ephesians 4:16). From the reception of these charisms or gifts, including those which are less dra-

[1] Thomas, Aquinas, *Summa Theologica*, Volume 1, Question III, "Of the Division of Grace," (New York: Benziger Brothers, Inc., 1947) pp. 1138–1139.

matic, there arises for each believer the right and duty to use them in the Church and in the world for the good of mankind and for the upbuilding of the Church.

Jesus himself tells his apostles at the end of Mark's Gospel:

> Go into the whole world and preach the gospel to all creation. He who believes and is baptized will be saved; but he who does not believe will be condemned. And these signs will accompany those who believe: in my name they will cast out demons; they will speak in new tongues; they will pick up serpents and if they drink any deadly thing, it will not hurt them; they will lay their hands on the sick and they will recover. Mark 16:15–18

Therefore, through the power of God's intervention in his Spirit, many are coming again to expect the manifestation of the spiritual gifts. God's Church does need to be renewed, nay, restored and it is only the infinite, just and saving power of God which can do it as he works through our human surrender and cooperation.

More specifically, as Paul develops in 1 Corinthians, these gifts are primarily given to build the Christian community. They are not given just for an individual's private/personal growth in the Christian life. The seven fold gifts of the Spirit we studied as children *are* given to build our personal relationship with God and to prepare us individually to be witnesses. But the nine gifts Paul speaks above in Corinthians are, as he says, to be *manifestations* of the Holy Spirit. They are to show forth his presence, his power among the people of God in order that the community of Christians may have all the necessary tools to be formed into the Body of Jesus Christ.

Let me explain what I mean in greater detail.

Note the first two gifts Paul mentions which are the utterance of wisdom and the utterance of knowledge.

The utterance of wisdom here referred to means wisdom teaching on how to live according to the Father's will. Steve Clark, again in his booklet, *Spiritual Gifts*, gives some excellent examples of this gift of practical spiritual teaching. When Christ spoke in response to the rich man's question and advised him to sell his possessions and follow him (Mark 10:20)—that was an utterance of wisdom. When Peter spoke in the Council of Jerusalem and declared that the Gentiles should not have to abide by the Mosaic Law on circumcision, that was wisdom from the mind of God.

The gift of the utterance of knowledge, on the other hand, refers to a deep understanding of God himself and the mysteries of God. It is a gift in which the mind is inspired (the Spirit breathes into) and a human person grasps a revelation of God and of his life among us which, when shared, raises the whole community to a new level of lived truth. It is sheer gift—not to be acquired by long hours of prayer and study though such preparation may open our minds and hearts to receive such a gift.

Both gifts, it is obvious, are given for the edification of the many.

Clark speaks of the next three gifts listed in Corinthians as sign gifts—that is, they are signs of God's power at work to bring all men and women to himself. "And I, if I be lifted up, will draw all men to myself." "When men see the power of God do something extraordinary, they do wonder and they do turn to God."[2]

When Paul speaks in this context about a gift of faith as a manifestation of the Spirit, it would appear that he

[2] *Ibid.*, p. 119

is speaking of a very special working of faith—that is, the gift to know *when* God desires to effect some wonder, to pray with unlimited confidence and experience the extraordinary results. Several years ago when the evangelist Kathryn Kuhlman was conducting a weekly service in Pittsburgh, I attended a few times and watched this gift at work. It is that gift of which Christ speaks:

> Truly I say to you, whoever says to this mountain "Be taken up and cast into the sea" and does not doubt in his heart but believes that what he says will come to pass, it will be done for him. Mark 11:23

She knew *when God* was *inspiring* her to pray for healing, or to pray for a change of heart among his people. That is the most important part of this gift—it is God-given. We cannot psyche ourselves up to receive this gift of faith, we cannot just pray for what we want to see happen, even if it appears good, but those with this gift can teach us *how* to pray and then we will witness the mighty works of God.

When people are living in committed relationships in a Christian context, there is an almost daily experience of the healing power of God. But there are those people who have been given special gifts of healing—gifts that operate more consistently and more dramatically than that found in the daily life of the Christian community. Such persons have been gifted so that those who do not know Christ may come to see and believe and that others in the mysterious workings of God's plan may be drawn closer to him. Father Francis MacNutt, O.P., and Sister Breige McKenna are perhaps the best known Catholics whom God has so gifted. At times such gifts of healing are used by God to effect what even our advanced medical knowledge would have to term miracles. Such is the goodness of a merciful God to a stiff-necked and stubborn generation. Even through my own life, while I do not believe God chooses to use me in a consistent way in this ministry, extraordinary healings have occured.

In November, 1969, I attended a Full Gospel Businessmen's meeting in Greensburg, Pennsylvania. Father MacNutt was the featured speaker for the evening and the chairman placed me at the head table beside Francis. At the end of the program Francis announced that he and I would pray for people in a side room. I had never prayed for healing so I informed Francis that I would stay beside him. When he began to pray for the first person, a woman who had suffered a tragic marriage and divorce, Francis became completely engrossed in her situation. I stood next to him for as long as I could but I kept glancing at over fifty people waiting patiently for prayer. Finally, I summoned up courage and approached them one at a time. The first few asked for spiritual graces and gifts but then I came upon a man who questioned me: "Do you minister prayer for healing?" I replied, "No." He said, "Do you believe in God's healing power?" I said, "Yes". He continued, "Will you pray for me?" I replied, "Yes, but I don't know whether anything will happen." He responded that he sensed God telling him to have a priest pray for his hearing. He explained to me that he had just been discharged from work. He was retired as legally deaf, and could hear only slightly out of one ear. I said, "OK, let's pray." I placed my fingers in his ears and prayed: Lord Jesus, heal my brother, restore his hearing." I continued to pray in tongues for a few seconds when suddenly I experienced a sense of power similar to electricity going through my hands and the two fingers I had placed in his ears. The man also experienced the power for he sat up suddenly and his eyes quickly looked into mine. I became uncomfortable and felt very awkward. What would I do if he were healed? I quickly said "Amen" and scurried across the room to a woman who was waiting for prayer.

Three months later I was driving through Pittsburgh with some Franciscan brothers of mine. We had heard there was a prayer meeting at St. Paul's Monastery and decided to go to it. Deep within me was a spiritual conviction that it was very important for me to be there, though I could not explain it logically. When we arrived, the meeting was well underway. I found an empty seat and sat down. No sooner had I done so when several rows in front of me, a man stood up with his back to me and began to witness that his hearing had been completely restored one evening six months before when a Catholic priest had prayed for him in Greensburg, Pennsylvania. The doctor, he said, had called it a miracle for his irreparably damaged ear drum was completely "new." He had come to this prayer meeting, he said, to witness to this healing and to ask forgiveness of all Catholics.

For years he had spoken against Catholics and carried hatred in his heart. But when God healed him through the priest he knew he was called to repent and glorify God by attempting to heal the damage he had caused.

On another occasion I visited my brother's family where their youngest child, Darlene, whom I had baptized, had recently been diagnosed as deaf. They had been to many doctors and various clinics but they were told it was a permanent condition. She was only months old and as I sat there listening to my brother and his wife, I knew a strong conviction from the Lord to go and pray. A few years of experience had taught me to be obedient to the Lord's direction on healing. I slipped into her room where she slept, anointed her with oil and celebrated the Sacrament of the Sick. During that time I experienced a strong sense of God's loving power going through me.

Two weeks later my brother in leaving his daughter's room accidently slammed the door. The child jumped and cried. Doctors verified that the child's hearing was not only normal but above normal.

I cite these examples to show that God works through whom he wills and when he wills for his own purposes. But he does want to heal and restore even when his human channels are reluctant or fearful.

This is an appropriate place to mention something on deliverance. Deliverance is that action taken to bind from interference or to cast out Satan or evil spirits under Satan's power. It is distinguished from exorcism which is the proper term for that action by which a possessed person is freed. Exorcism is a formal rite of the Church which must be specifically authorized by the local bishop in whose jurisdiction the rite will be discharged.

Deliverance, then, is an informal action done for less serious cases called oppression and obsession. Oppression refers to the interference of evil from the outside usually manifested in an external pressing in upon thought processes and one's general disposition. It usually comes about because of some direct contact that the individual has had with the activity of evil spirits. This contact may be accidental as coming into a gathering of people involved in occult practices. In the case of oppression, a general command in Jesus' Name for the oppressing or interfering spirit to leave is usually sufficient.

Obsession involves some binding force of evil in one part of a person's life. Thus, one having given in to a tantrum and rage might find that he is under the influence of a spirit of rage or hatred. Usually, if he commands that spirit in the name of Jesus to depart, he will be free. He may, in a given instance, need to have another Christian exercise this authority with him.

I briefly mention this large area of deliverance first, because it is closely related to healing. Many times, especially in the case of healing the inner person, for example, a healing from feelings of worthlessness, what is necessary before praying for God's Spirit of love to heal the person is first to command the spirit of self-condemnation in the name of Jesus to depart from that person. It is also true that the presence of evil spirits can block physical healing. This area needs substantial discernment in each instance since, more commonly, there are physical causes for illness which respond to medical treatment and prayer for healing.

The second reason for mentioning deliverance here is that deliverance is an accepted ministry in charismatic renewal. It would be negligent to give an overview of the renewal without mentioning it. Despite its acceptance it is in an early stage of development and this ministry requires much pastoral wisdom and guidance. As Christians come to see once again the importance of deliverance and learn to integrate it into daily Christian life, it is salutary for all of us to reflect on the words of Pope Paul VI:

Evil is not merely a deficiency, it is the act of a live, spiritual, perverted and perverting being. A terrible, mysterious and fearful reality. Those who refuse to recognize his existence . . . or who present him as a pseudo reality, a fabrication of the mind serving to personify the unknown causes of our evils, are departing from the teaching of the Bible and the Church.[3]

The last four gifts cited by Paul in his letter Clark terms revelational gifts—that is, through these gifts God makes known to his people his mind, his will on a present situation or a need for direction among his people.

The gift of prophecy is a means God uses to speak to a third person but more often to a whole community. He desires to show us his mind on a current situation and often the direction he wishes us to take. The more the prophet yields to God, the more pure can his word be given. Prophecy does not reveal new truths. Revelation is complete but prophecy does interpret God's revealed truths for our present situation and give direction on what is to be done. Such a gift is to be tested over and over but once confirmed by the Christian community as truly in accord with the teaching of scripture and the living tradition of the Church, it is to be embraced and seen as a means of knowing God's will within a committed body of people.

Bruce Yocum in his book, *Prophecy*, Word of Life (Servant Books, Ann Arbor, 1976), gives the most comprehensive treatment available on the role of prophecy in the Church today. He deals with the difficulties in exercising the prophetic gift and the caution necessary to avoid false prophecy and non-prophecy. He uses as a model for today's church the five prophetic actions recorded in the Acts of the Apostles. The first is the prophetic prediction of Agabus that a famine would soon come to the whole world (Acts 11). This prophecy enabled the Christians to be prepared at the time the

[3] Osservatore Romano, Nov. 16, 1972.

famine began. Second was the confirmation of the prophets at Antioch that Barnabas and Paul should be sent as missionaries (Acts 13). The third prophetic instance did not involve a prediction of the future or a directive action but rather an inspirational discourse. Judas and Silas prophesied so as to encourage and strengthen the disciples at Antioch (Acts 15). This form of prophecy which inspires the hearers to deeper faith is the most common form of prophecy in the charismatic renewal.

In Acts 21 we find two more prophetic instances, both involving warnings to Paul. The first warned Paul not to go to Jerusalem. In the second case Agabus, the prophet we referred to in Acts 11, now tells Paul how the Jews will bind him and hand him over to the Gentiles.

Christians prophesied regularly when they came together (1 Cor. 11:4–5, 14:3). Prophecy is listed frequently as one of the gifts Christ bestows on the Church (Romans 12:6; Ephesians 4:11–12; 1 Corinthians 12:10, 28, 29). Prophets are listed immediately after Apostles in the foundation ministries of the Church (Eph. 2:20). Christians are encouraged to value prophecy (1 Thess. 5:20) and to seek it more earnestly than the other gifts (1 Cor. 14:1).

The charismatic renewal is striving to rediscover the right place for the prophetic ministry in the life of the Church. During the past twelve years prophecy has been a source of strength and encouragement for those first involved in the renewal to continue on despite difficulties. It has served to deepen the prayer and lift the spirits at many prayer meetings and conferences. It has been the basis for extensive efforts to strengthen individual lives and relationships in order to be prepared for times of difficulty expected for the church and the world.

Discernment or the gift to distinguish among spirits is a gift given to protect the life of God's people. Those persons having this gift from God exercise it by determining whether God's Spirit, a human spirit or the evil one himself is a work in a particular person's actions or in a situation. Those in the Christian community treasure this gift in a particular way because it safeguards their own gifts, their relationships and the direction of the community to which they have committed their lives. It is through this gift, given to a number of people, that the work *God* wants accomplished by a particular community can be focused on and not on a number of other good works.

Speaking in tongues or praying in tongues—which is a way I like to refer to this gift since it is a gift of *prayer*—can be used in two different ways. First, it can be a gift of prayer used by an individual in his/her private prayer with God (1 Cor. 14:5; 1 Cor. 14:14). Secondly, this gift is given for the upbuilding of the whole body when the Spirit urges a person to pray aloud in tongues in the assembly. Yet, as Paul so well says when the gift is used this way, it must also be followed by interpretation:

> If any speak in a tongue, let there be only two or at most three, and each in turn; and let one interpret. But if there is no one to interpret let each of them keep silence in Church and speak to himself and God. 1 Cor. 14:27

Interpretation of tongues is a gift much like prophecy. It is not a translation of a language one knows but an inspiration from God to interpret the prayer of the Spirit.

All of us by Baptism are temples of the Holy Spirit

and the prayer of the Spirit—tongues—is the Spirit of God praising through us to the Father. It is sheer gift to be able to enter into that stream of living water—that fountain of praise rising up from deep within us.

When others are gifted to interpret that praise, that word of prayer for us, it is a sign of the unity of the one Spirit in his Body.

For those not involved in charismatic renewal the gift of tongues understandably impresses them as a curious and striking phenomenon. We have been trained to treat as suspect anything which bypasses our rational faculties. Yet those who pray in tongues find that the value lies not in the gift for its own sake but in experiencing it as a means of enabling deeper union with God. It is a language of love, a language leading to more intimate inclusion in the family of God.

That is why those involved in charismatic renewal have little to say when asked about tongues itself. Our focus and attention are on our relationship with God and only secondarily on the "language" which expresses that relationship. Nevertheless, because it is a gift of God, it is a precious treasure and a cause for rejoicing when it has been given.[1]

The gifts here described are most commonly used in a prayer meeting which is a weekly gathering in either denominational or ecumenical groups of those Chris-

[1] While the purpose of this book does not include an exhaustive study of the gifts but rather an overview of them, readers may be interested in pursuing study further, particularly on the gift of tongues, through the following books: Rene Laurentin. *Catholic Pentecostalism.* translated by Matthew J. O'Connell. Garden City: Doubleday and Company, Inc., 1977; Kilian McDonnell, O.S.B. *Charismatic Renewal and the Churches.* New York: Seabury Press, 1976; John Sherrill. *They Speak with Other Tongues.* New York: Pyramid Books, 1965.

tians who desire to know the full power of the Spirit working in their lives.

These gatherings have as their purpose to worship and praise God under the direction of the Holy Spirit and to build up the Christian lives of one another by the use of the gifts. These meetings were part of the daily life of the early church. Paul, again in his letter to the Corinthians, chapters twelve to fourteen, teaches the brethren how to conduct themselves and to use their gifts at these gatherings.

Such a meeting usually includes prolonged periods of worship, prayer and song. Interspersed in the meeting will be the reading of appropriate Scripture, sharing on the Word of God and witnessing to the goodness of God in people's lives. Usually, the leader of the prayer meeting or some other member with necessary gifts will teach on the Word of God or some practical way to grow in the Christian life.

During such gatherings, people will learn to use and mature in the use of gifts.

Before and after the prayer meeting are often times for additional teaching in growing in the use of gifts, ministries and the Christian life in general. In addition, at these times the Life in the Spirit Seminars are held to instruct those desiring to give their lives more deeply to the Lord and experience the full release of his Holy Spirit. Finally, at the conclusion of the meeting persons with gifts in counseling, intercessory prayer and healing will minister to those in need.

These meetings concentrate on praise and the Word of God. They are paraliturgical in nature which means they are intended to support the Eucharistic Liturgy and not replace it. They are times for the People of God to grow together in worship through an informal and usually spontaneous response to the leading of the Holy

Spirit. In nearly every instance where people have regularly participated in prayer meetings they have found that the quality of their worship and general participation at Mass and other sacramental celebrations have improved. The free structure of the prayer meeting allows for immediate response to inspiration and therefore it tends to be a more enthusiastic gathering than a liturgical assembly. It also tends to be uneven in pace and quality. There are times when it is fast moving and other times when the readings, witnessing and prayer seem slow and heavy. There are moments when the power of God's Word seems overwhelming and other times when what is said appears to most to be nice reflections which are neither insightful nor anointed. All of this contrasts with the Eucharistic Liturgy in which the order is usually the same. The prayer meeting could become a testing ground for the exercise of the spiritual gifts which could then be exercised within the liturgical assembly. It is reasonable to forsee a time when the prayer meeting serves as the major instrument for increasing the vitality and spiritual power of the liturgies. This would presume not just the growth in maturity and reliability of spiritual gifts and ministries but a corresponding growth in the communal character of the assembly.

This area of prayer meetings and communal development will be better understood in light of the following chapter which will deal with what should be the normal Christian life and celebration of the sacraments in the Church.

Father Michael Scanlan. TOR. speaks to participants at the beginning of one of the Conference liturgies.

Bishop Raymond Lucker from Minnesota addresses conferees in the tent.

Father Scanlan served as general Chairman at the Priests' Conference on Catholic Charismatic Renewal at Steubenville, Ohio.

Photos: Christian Conference College of Steubenville

Father Scanlan meets with bishops attending the Conference. Left to right. Bishop George M. Pearce, SM. of the Fiji Islands; Bishop Albert Ottenweiler. Steubenville; Bishop Raymond Lucker, New Ulm, Minn.; Bishop Eugene Gerber. Dodge City. Kans.; Auxiliary Bishop Paul V. Dudley. St. Paul-Minneapolis; Auxiliary Bishop Joseph A. Ferrario of Honolulu.

Father Francis Martin concelebrates Mass with Father John Bertolucci.

Priests move in procession to the tent for the celebration of the liturgy of the Priests' Conference on Catholic Charismatic Renewal. The group headquarters is in the College of Steubenville, Steubenville, Ohio.

A portion of the tent in which priests gathered for the opening of the Conference for Priests on Charismatic Renewal in the Catholic Church.

Small groups of priests meet to share with and minister to one another.

Father Francis MacNutt, O.P., gives a homily during one of the Priests' Conference Masses.

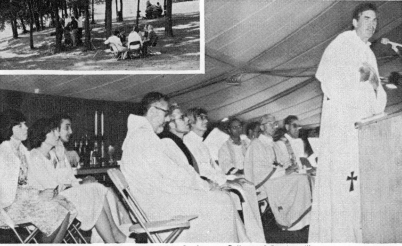

Photos: Christian Conference College of Steubenville

1,000 clergy discuss what's 'normal churc

"What came out very early was that the first step evangelization is the spiritual renewal of the priesthood," said Father Brendan Dalton of Epiphany Parish, Miami, reflecting on the Fourth National Catholic Charismatic Conference for Priests and Deacons held at the College of Steubenville, Ohio.

Nine other priests from the Archdiocese were part of 1,000 clergy and hierarchy from the United States and 15 countries ...

What Is Normal Church Life, Priests Ask

The 951 ordained persons attending the fourth annual National Catholic Charismatic Conference for Priests and Deacons here were told by the keynote speaker that "it takes strong leadership to decentralize" the Church, but that "it's either decentralize or disintegrate."

On the hilly campus of the College of Steubenville the priests, deacons and ... from 48 states and 20 countries ... to hear discussed ... in our

them for change. We priests haven't begun to tap our potential resources. What is called for first of all, though, is our own personal conversion."

He said that every liturgy should be an evangelical experience and that social issues "can't possibly be faced until we grow in an awareness of Jesus Christ."

The priests heard an Idaho colleague recently returned from Latin America relate his experiences in an inner city parish setting "not too much unlike ... own."

... William Weigand, former ... he earned

Bishops in attendance at the conference met with Father Michael Sc... with back to camera) prior to the Mass which they were asked to co... with Bishop McKinney (right, speaking) the principal celebrant. O... include retired Bishop George H. Pearce, SM, of the Fiji Island... Bishop Ottenweiler, Bishop Lucker, Bishop Eugene ... Paul V. Dudley of St. Paul-Minneapo... ... A. Ferrario of Honolu...

Exuberant Liturgy Of The Conference

Priests Give Public Testimony Of Faith

FRATERNITY. Fellow priests share a silent moment of prayer during the third annual National Conference For Priests on the Catholic Charismatic Renewal at the College of Steubenville campus. The campus drew priests from around the country and several (Herald-Star George)

Conference Has Big Influence

By BILL O'CONNOR
Herald-Star Staff Writer

The charismatic movement for spiritual renewal within the Catholic Church continues to grow and the influence of The College of Steuben ...

But those conferences now have grown well beyond the sole influence of any one man. What the priests have found here, each year, they say, is fellowship ...

CHAPTER FIVE

THE NORMAL CHRISTIAN LIFE

It's a simple, sometimes patched and multicolored circus tent in which the Priests' Conference on Catholic Charismatic Renewal is conducted every year at the College of Steubenville since 1975. Why a tent? There are no indoor facilities large enough on campus to hold the one thousand or so priests and deacons who attend the week-long conference. But in that humble dwelling the priests have experienced God. They have frequently related the experience to a passage in the book of Exodus:

> Then the cloud covered the meeting tent and the glory of the Lord filled the Dwelling. Moses could not enter the meeting tent because the cloud settled down upon it and the glory of the Lord filled the Dwelling. Exodus 40:34–35

Sometimes in heavy rain and mud, sometimes in heat intensified under the canvas, sometimes in a gentle breeze, God has spoken his word in extraordinary power. It is obvious that God desires to heal, strengthen and empower his shepherds. Those men have been a rich source of encouragement and Christian witness to me as

they open to God, humble themselves before one another, seek forgiveness, step out in faith to proclaim the
goodness and mercy of God to those whom the Lord has
placed under their care. Such has been our experience of
these conferences and they are anticipated with great
eagerness by the community here which volunteers its
services for the week.

On the opening night of the 1978 Conference as I addressed the nine hundred and fifty one participants, including eight bishops, I spoke of how I had yearned for a
conference on this theme: The Normal Christian Life in
the Local Church. So much that had been said at earlier
conferences could now be put into perspective. We could
proclaim the deepest desires of our hearts to live according to the Gospel norms in a normal Christian-Catholic
way. We weren't seeking a movement, an individualized
expression of Christianity and, least of all, a club. We
wanted to live the normal life according to the Word of
God revealed to us in Scripture and tradition. We desired to take and live this inheritance.

Father Francis Martin, a priest from Madonna House
in Combermere, Ontario and a professor at the Ecole
Biblique in Jerusalem, who holds a doctorate in Scripture from the Biblicum in Rome, gave the first main
address. Francis developed the characteristics of the
normal Christian life. He listed them as: 1) knowing
Jesus personally and giving our lives to him; 2) living in
a conscious awareness of the power of the Holy Spirit; 3)
living in local community; 4) bearing fruit in service,
particularly evangelism; 5) communities interacting in
unity with one another. His talk developed an approach
that had been increasingly effective in giving Catholics
clarity on the goals of the renewal. The charismatic renewal was indeed intended to restore the normal or
normative state of Church life as prescribed in the gospel and reflected in New Testament Church life. These

five characteristics summarize five main thrusts of the renewal and put in perspective the reason behind the points emphasized in the teaching and preaching in charismatic renewal. Because of the importance of these characteristics in understanding the existing state of the renewal and its probable future development, they will be explained in some detail.

"First," he said, "we need to know Jesus as our Lord. We need to know Jesus personally and give our entire lives to him." Paul says in Galatians 1:16 that God "chose to reveal his son to *me*." Later in chapter two he says, "I still live my human life but it is a life of faith in the Son of God who loved *me* and gave himself up for *me*." (My italics.) Paul knew Jesus. He knew him personally not because Paul was an extraordinary man but because he embraced Jesus as his Lord and Savior. We make the same verbal confession today but we act as though God's intimacy with man was reserved to those involved in the beginning of the church. If Jesus died and rose for each of us—if he had that kind of personal love for us, does it not make sense that he would want to speak to us and direct our lives? It is true that there are many ways he does speak to us: through the teaching of the Church; wisdom of men and women whose religious convictions we trust; through circumstances and events. But it is equally true that he speaks clearly and personally in the minds and hearts of those who seek him in truth.

Paul says "God chose to reveal his Son to *me*." Paul knew he was loved—what about us? Are we ready to seek him with purity of heart, divest ourselves of those things which keep us from hearing him clearly? Are we ready to proclaim him Lord over our lives?

> . . . at the name of Jesus every knee should bow, in heaven and on earth and under the earth, and every tongue con-

fess Jesus Christ is Lord, to the glory of God the Father.
Philippians 2:10–11

Paul also says "No one can say Jesus is Lord except by
the Holy Spirit." (1 Cor. 12:3) We could say without
understanding: "That's silly—I can say it. Jesus is
Lord." But what Paul is saying is that only in the power
of the Spirit can we die to ourselves and submit to a
living Lordship which by the gospel paradox leads to
freedom.

The first act of the Holy Spirit in those who have
opened their lives to the fullness of his direction is to
give us the heart of Jesus so that we can cry "Abba!
Father! Daddy! My Abba!" The first role of the Holy
Spirit is to put us in right relationship to Jesus and the
Father. Jesus is our Lord and brother. He is our way to
the Father. The first act of the Holy Spirit is to reveal
that to us for our personal lives. "All who are led by the
Spirit of God are sons of God. You did not receive a
spirit of slavery leading you back into fear, but a spirit
of adoption through which we cry out "Abba!" (that is,
Father). Romans 8:14–15.

A second characteristic of the normal Christian life is
to live in conscious awareness of the power of the Holy
Spirit. This is not just a belief in the presence of the Holy
Spirit because we are taught it. Rather it is a knowledge
of the presence of the Holy Spirit not just dwelling but
empowering our lives. The initial experience of this em-
powerment is usually referred to as "being baptized in
the Holy Spirit." We should normally know the power of
the Spirit to lead us in prayer, guide us in our lives and
minister through us to others. Through the conscious
presence of the Spirit we are given the gifts described in
Chapter 3. We are going down a blind alley if we think
that we, with our good programs, good ideas and good

will, can renew the Church. Only God can. We are called to learn his plan, his way and be obedient to it. While we are responsible to use our gifts and talents, nevertheless, they are to be put at the service of God's plan. We have to stop asserting that we think we have a better idea. We've been doing this for too long and as statistics show us only one in four persons in the world indicates any kind of belief in Jesus.

We need apostles, prophets, teachers, pastors, preachers and healers who know Jesus and are empowered with these gifts by His Spirit.

But such gifts can be truly confirmed and called forth in their fullness only through community—the third characteristic of the normal Christian life.

Scripture tells us there is one Lord, one faith, one baptism, one God and Father of us all who is over all and in all and through all. Our lives should reflect that unity through a network of committed relationships. We are called to such committed relationships within the local church so that we might help one another to be saints; that we might enable one another to respond to the Lord Jesus with all we have.

If there is no clear commitment to one another, no clear agreements on how to care for one another, there is no community. Primary agreements are not to rules and regulations but to *one another* that we might be saints.

It is not normal for Christians to live isolated, individualized or alienated lives.

One problem today in the Church is that there is so little community. Our parishes are so large, strangers sit next to strangers at Sunday Mass. We gather together for fund raising events and that's fine as far as it goes but we need to be gathered to share one another's human lives in a regular way. Look at Scripture: Paul presupposes the normal Christian life in community. He writes to communities. He speaks to communities. The fullness of God's word through Paul is only understood in light of community.

> And all who believed were together and had all things in common; and they sold their possessions and goods and distributed them to all as any had need. And day by day attending the temple together and breaking bread in their homes they partook of food with glad and generous hearts, praising God and having favor with all the people. And the Lord added to their number day by day those who were being saved." Acts 2:43–47

It is important to say something here about authority and gifts in light of committed relationships. Authority is not vested in just one function. Leadership, that is, directive authority, is necessary and good to the life of the body. But if we see this form of authority as making our weight felt, as having a title, we are clearly not seeing it as Christ intended. Scripture clearly tells us, "It shall not be so among you." (Mt. 20:26) To serve one another, to be the least in having needs satisfied, to wash one another's feet—that's exercising authority from the position of the Master. But from this humble attitude those in authority *are to serve the Lord*—his truth, his wisdom, his love, his will, his plan are to be followed, not the whims of those they serve. And those in authority are accountable to God to have led in the way of truth. "Obey your leaders and submit to them: for they are keeping watch over your souls, as men who will have to give account." (Hebrews 13:17)

There are many other levels of authority that flow from the gifts of the Spirit. When a person's gifts are integrated clearly within the body of Christ, then prophets, preachers, teachers, healers, musicians, evangelizers have authority from Jesus Christ within the sphere of that gift to bring his life, his truth, his transforming power to people's lives.

The concept of authority is confused today in the Church because the gifts are not confirmed and operative within each local Church. We have abdicated our personal responsibility for the growth of the body through our gifts and literally dumped it all on the directive authority of the Church in such a way that this authority has had to shoulder a burden God never intended it to carry. If all parts of the body were exercising their gifts to build the body of Jesus Christ; if we were supporting and protecting one another including our leaders, in truth and love, there would be little opportunity for authority to get out of hand, to be misused from self-gain or from insecurity.

We need to give one another authority according to the gifts we have received. We need to be able to go to those confirmed in leadership by the Church, to those with gifts of wisdom and discernment and say "Speak to me of God's will, tell me what it is you believe He wants for my life"—and seriously take to heart what we hear. When we can do that in freedom, many parts of the Body of Christ will begin to operate again.

The fourth characteristic of the normal Christian life is to show forth fruits of service to all God's children, primarily through evangelism. A Christian should bear fruit, should care for the poor, should shoulder others' burdens and most of all, be so filled with the good news of the Gospel that he witnesses to it regularly to others. The normal state of the Christian community is that it is growing through evangelism. Our greatest service therefore to the poor, the sick, the alienated is to evangelize them with power—a power that changes lives. We need to be able to say: "You can live a life that makes sense—here—come and see."

Why hasn't this happened? Because quite simply, we too often fail to obey Him and to have a pure heart, that is, to be single-hearted in following his will. We have succumbed to the tyranny of the urgent. We spread ourselves out under our own power and falsely assume that if there's a clear pressing need that will effect good, God wants us to do it.

Instead, we are called to come before the Lord, humble ourselves, place our agenda before Him and submit to the priority of the *important* from God's perspective.

His first priority based on his word is that people be converted to Him and build committed relationships with one another. This is God's will in order that his people may show in word and deed their unity so that the world may believe Jesus came from the Father for the salvation of the world.

> I do not pray for these only, but also for those who believe in me through their word, that they may all be one; even as you, Father, are in me and I in you, that they also may be in us so that the world may believe that you have sent me. (John 17:20–21)

Finally, if we are living the Gospel life in committed relationships, then we should experience the fruit of our unity as Christ intended. "The Lord day by day added to their number those who were being saved." (Acts 2:47)

The fifth characteristic is communities relating to one another in mutual support and unity. No one community or parish is to be isolated. Each is to have a place in the Church and be relating to others as members of *one* Body. Francis did not develop this characteristic in detail because he said that today we need to concentrate on the first four, then with the renewed normal life we can consider and develop the fifth characteristic of the normal Christian life.

Following Francis Martin came Father John Bertolucci, noted evangelist and pastor of St. Joseph's Parish in Little Falls, New York. John spoke on how to bring people into that personal relationship with Jesus Christ. He gave many examples how priests and deacons could witness, preach and invite people into this new relationship. He continually remarked that this presumed that the priest or deacon was already in that relationship himself: "What is called for first of all though is our own personal conversion." He said that every liturgy should be an evangelical experience and that social issues "can't possibly be faced until we grow in an awareness of Jesus Christ."

Next came Father William Weigand, former Chancellor of the Boise, Idaho Diocese and for nine years, a missionary in Cali, Colombia. Bill gave practical illustrations from his parish experience of how a parish itself needs to be a community of communities. He spoke of his parish of fifty thousand which has broken into communities each headed by lay people. He and his associate had to launch thirty prayer communities in his parish and trust the leadership of uneducated laymen; it worked. The small communities met weekly apart from the Liturgy. "Real ministry is not parish-centered, but out there." (with the people) "It's not the pastor and staff's role to plan but to support and coordinate and share. Our principle was that whatever you have received from others you can share." Bill concluded by saying he is applying the same principles in his new parish in Homedale, Idaho.

The most unusual talk of the conference was given by Bishop Raymond Lucker of New Ulm, Minnesota and one of the three delegates from the United States to the 1977 Roman Synod. The conference was raised to a new level of expectancy as Bishop Lucker said it is not normal:

—when the bishop is financier, architect, engineer and when he makes all the decisions;

—when he does not delegate authority;

—to think of the local Church as the parish where Father does everything;

—for a priest to get rich from the offerings of the poor;

—for people to go to Church and not be converted;

—to know about Christ and not know Christ;

—when the great heroes of our day are on the Johnny Carson show and when Las Vegas is the great Mecca;

—when the logical instruction is taken to be catechesis and vast numbers of Catholics have never been evangelized;

—for the Chancery Office and not Jesus Christ to be the center of the diocese;

—when social action is centered exclusively in the political arena;

—when in the local Church, worship is dead, youth are turned off and what they came for (Jesus Christ) cannot be found.

Bishop Lucker spoke of his life living in a diocesan pastoral center in a community with a retired priest, three sisters and a layman, who is an administrative assistant. He stated that he, as the Shepherd, needs to live in community before preaching community to others.

For the first time in the Catholic Charismatic Renewal, a conference dealt with integrating community building and parish renewal. The charismatic renewal has experienced an ongoing tension between those who state that the only effective renewal is to begin in the parishes because that is where all the people are and that is the necessary basic unit of Church and those who say beginning at the parish level does not work; it is putting new wine in old wineskins. Some of the latter group holds that the independent community is the foundation stone for the total renewal.

This conference taught the necessary relationship between parishes and communities. The communities are similar to a first wave, a beachhead of renewal. The communities become models of normal Christian life as well as resource centers for those who can teach the formation necessary for establishing this life in the parishes. The conference seemingly inaugurated a new understanding of the respective places and interdependence of the community and parish renewal.

The effect of these talks and other homilies by the team was to free the nine hundred fifty one participants to commit themselves to be normal as Christians and to call those around them into this normal living in the freedom of "the sons of God." The priests and deacons departed, not to promote a movement, but to grab onto their inheritance as Christians, to proclaim it and build the Church according to gospel norms. They left with the freedom to say to their parishioners, students, fellow priests and bishops: "The Lord Jesus Christ is calling us to live the normal gospel life and I know what that life is and here is how we are going to normalize in our part of the Church."

The interrelationship of building community and renewing parishes is most strikingly present in the celebration of sacraments. The celebration of the seven sacraments is probably the most visible part of parish life.

With the Eucharist as most prominent, followed by Baptism, Confirmation and Matrimony as parish events and penance and anointing as important events in the lives of individuals and families, the sacraments, before all else, highlight and reveal parish life. Any discussion of normal Church life must therefore reflect on the normative way of celebrating the sacraments.

Since the book on the Sacraments[1] which I coauthored with Sr. Ann Therese Shields was published, I have had new opportunities of growing in the pastoral care of a faith community.

My experience of the past two years has revealed new power in very specific ways in the communal celebrations of the sacraments, particularly of Baptism and Marriage. Such experience has also provided all of us in the community with substantial insight regarding the relationship between community life, sacramental celebration and the normal Christian life just described.

There is a great emphasis among Catholics today on liturgical planning as the key to good liturgy. Parishes are urged to establish liturgy committees, to train the leaders, and to have the committees plan each liturgy in detail. It is common to hear liturgists speak of the power of liturgy to build community.

It is true that good liturgies can improve the communal life of the assembly. It is also true that liturgical committees can be an effective tool for improving liturgies. Nevertheless, there is a deeper truth: that the spiritual state of the community is a crucial and limiting force in liturgical celebration. Liturgy is the celebration of community, and the extent to which there is community under the lordship of Jesus Christ will determine the potential for communal celebration.

[1] Scanlan and Shields, *And Their Eyes Were Opened: Encountering Jesus in the Sacraments* (Ann Arbor: Servant Books, 1976)

Furthermore, each sacrament is directly related to the community in a particular way, and therefore, the state of the community will determine the specific fruit of the sacrament.

In the sacraments of initiation which Catholics have traditionally recognized as Baptism, Confirmation, and the Eucharist, the Christian community welcomes new members, new brothers and sisters. Thus, specifically in Baptism, the community is called to pray by the rite for the newly baptized and receive him or her into the communal life. The more there is a community, joined in mind and heart under the lordship of Jesus, the greater will be the power of the prayer. To the extent that the community is sharing life and has achieved maturity, to that extent will the newly initiated member be able to live a shared Christian life. In other words, to use an image, if the community has, by the power of God, reached a spiritual depth of 5°, then the new member can be assured of support in his or her Christian life at that level. But if the community has grown to a spiritual level of 25°, then the newly initiated can be formed and supported into life at that depth.

Too often have the sacraments of initiation been seen only in the *individual* dimension of enabling Christians to grow in the new life of Jesus Christ. In particular, Baptism does effect a transformation of persons into sons and daughters of God, brothers and sisters in the Lord, and temples of the Holy Spirit. This effect is pledged by God to those who will come to be baptized. This effect is called, in the Roman Catholic tradition, the "ex opere operato" power of the sacrament: the sacrament in itself creates the potential for a new way of living.

But the Christian community is to activate that new life, form it and nurture it to maturity. It makes a substantial difference whether one is baptized in a pagan environment and left to fend for oneself or one is baptized into a vital Christian community which takes responsibility for the new life.

We should see the sacrament of matrimony in much the same way. God has pledged his grace to those who join with one another in matrimony. There, a transformation occurs whereby two persons achieve a new identity with one another. They become not just a man and a woman joined together, but husband and wife. Their relationship as a married couple is intrinsically part of their identity before God.

But the support and direction this couple receives from a Christian community will have a substantial effect on how they live out their sacramental union. The level of married life in that community will be the level of life into which they can be initiated. If there is little spirituality and little support of families by other families and single people, then this new couple will receive little encouragement to grow into Christian maturity as a couple. If there is a great deal of loving interaction, if husbands help the recently married man grow as a husband and father, if wives help the recently married woman to grow as a wife and mother, and if this help comes from those who have grown in wisdom and holiness, then we can expect that the newly married will receive the support they need to mature into a strong Christian family.

It is also essential that the priest understand that the fruit of the sacraments depends in part on the recognition of his responsibility to pastor the whole community *while* it celebrates the sacraments. There is a tendency to execute Baptism and Marriage as functional ministries at worst or as a personal pastoring of individuals receiving the sacraments at best. In other words, there is a tendency to make Baptism and Marriage events in which a few people are the participants and the others present are observers.

Such an approach will not further the life of the community.

I base these observations on my experience in the past few years giving pastoral care to our faith community, the Servants of God's Love. Occasions of Baptism and Marriage are times when the entire community is present to recognize its identity as a faith community, assuming the burdens of its members and committing itself to new relationships. As a result, the liturgical aspect of the sacraments has become more powerful.

In infant baptism the community joins in the prayers of commitment made by the parents and godparents. As baptized Christians, the community with the pastor takes authority in praying for deliverance and exorcism so that the child, claimed for the kingdom of light, may live in full protection under the active guardianship of a community which recognizes its commitment to a dependent infant. Following the actual baptism, the community joyfully receives the newly-baptized as a sister or brother. I always hold a baby up high for all to see and present it as a new member of the Christian community. The community takes that child to its heart with shouts of gladness and applause.

Later in the rite of Baptism, I pray with the whole community for the inner healing of the child and the parents. These prayers are intended to heal the emotions and the body from any trauma suffered during pregnancy and birth. Finally, at the end of Mass the community joins in a prayer of blessing over the mother and the father and again commits itself to support the Christian life of the new child of God.

This joyous celebration is not simply the result of

planning. It is the natural expression of a community of Christians whose lives are joined in deep commitment to the Lord and to each other.

The ceremony is surrounded by signs of this communal life. When a child is born, women will offer to cook meals for the new mother and care for other children in the family. Such acts of generosity clearly say, "We are glad this child has come into the world and we want to help in caring for it."

Often members of the community are chosen as godparents for the new child and will thus have a very special role in preparing for the baptism. Others will participate in planning the actual service and the community celebration following it.

Our experiences have similarly demonstrated the vital role community plays in the sacrament of Marriage. Too often today a man and woman are married within the Church but believe they are to make it on their own. Only if there is a serious problem do they sometimes approach a pastor for help. But we believe no Christian married couple is expected to handle alone all their emotional and financial burdens or the care and Christian growth of their children. God intends that they have brothers and sisters to support, love and upbuild them. The community's commitment strengthens their marriage bond and it not only frees the couple from isolation in serious difficulty but enables them to grow as man and woman in love and wisdom for their own lives and their children.

In our community, we have small pastoral groups set up according to sex and state in life. The purpose of these groups, composed of five to eight people, is to provide a small number of brothers and sisters who can offer direct daily love and wisdom. Weekly meetings provide for sharing life and being accountable to brothers and sisters for the use of the gifts and graces of God. As one of the expressions of their love for one another, these groups help their members prepare for marriage.

In preparation for marriage, couples will also offer counseling, wisdom and care as appropriate. Pastoral groups to which the man and woman belong will host wedding showers and bachelor parties. Finally, such groups often help in planning the actual wedding and participating in it. The whole community will be involved in providing for the wedding reception.

All of these acts are concrete signs to the couple that they have brothers and sisters saying to their union, saying with their lives, that they will be with them in all that is ahead.

Another expression of community commitment takes place during the actual celebration of the sacrament. Frequently, members of the community in accordance with their positions in the community take the principal roles in the marriage ceremony. Thus, the principal pastor of the community will be the main celebrant with the priest who prepared the couple for marriage as the chief concelebrant. The lay leaders of the community will participate in prayers for the newly married couple. Members of the bride and groom's pastoral groups will often be in the wedding party. Those having musical and prophetic ministries will be present to exercise their gifts. The whole community will join in spontaneous praise at the peak moments of celebration and as a community will extend hands and pray over the couple for the richest blessings of God.

After the couple's honeymoon, the community is there in the pastoral groups and in many other ways to encourage and support them.

The third sacrament which I would like to dwell on at

some length is the Eucharist. The Eucharist is the primary event in the life of the Church. It is primary in the sense of celebrating the dying and the rising of the Lord and therefore the source of the Christian life. It is primary in the sense of sustaining; it provides the Bread of Life both in the Word of God proclaimed and the Body and Blood consumed. It is primary in the sense of expressing most clearly the communal nature of the local Body of Christ gathered to worship and celebrate this unity in the Lord.

Everything that is involved in charismatic renewal and most especially the development of community has direct application in the Eucharist. The power to praise is given voice with the opening song and the acclamation of the Gloria in the liturgy. The convicting power of the Holy Spirit is what can empower the penitential rite to effect conversion of heart and to heal wounds of the inner man. The anointing of the Spirit enables the lectors of the scripture readings to proclaim with power. The celebrant's growth in the Spirit of God will enable him to break open the Word of scripture so that what he preaches is not just good instruction which is well-chosen for the parish, not just well prepared scriptural exegesis which is vividly illustrated, not just well delivered according to the best style of homiletics, *but* it is the Spirit-empowered fresh word that makes the scriptures a "today word," a "living word" feeding the people. The key element in preaching is to release the Spirit from the inspired Word of God. The Old and the New Testament are words of men which are also the Word of God because the Holy Spirit has been breathed into them. The preacher needs to be knowledgeable about scripture, he needs to develop his speaking ability, he needs to prepare himself and his understanding of the Word but he needs most of all to rely on the life-giving power of the living Word. He needs, as Francis of Assisi instructed, to grow hot with the cold written word of God so that he might present it to his people as a living word for their lives today. In personal prayer he will learn to know the lead of the Spirit as to the particular emphasis and focus on the Word which will release such power for the people. If the preacher breaks open the bread of life in the Word, he will have a congregation with an increased understanding of their identity and prepared to join him in breaking the Bread of Life in the Eucharist.

The Spirit strengthens us to go beyond our natural limitations and daily temptations to anxiety and fear. When the Word of God is preached in power, the people are prepared for new commitment and self-sacrifice. The proclamation of the Creed is a time for commitment. The prayers of the faithful and the offertory are times for committed self-sacrifice in prayer and action for the Church and neighbor. (The prayers of the faithful presume common concerns and the offertory common ownership of the gifts).

When the Liturgy of the Word has freed the congregation to move beyond the daily constrictions of life, the people are ready to join with the priest and the Lord in the most powerful prayer ever celebrated: the dying and rising of Jesus in the Consecration of the Mass. If the right preparation has been made, the people can be called into the deepest quiet, the most solemn and reverential posture of worship and the closest experience to the eternal now that man can know in this life as the celebrant proclaims: "This is MY BODY which will be given up for you"; "This is the cup of my blood, the blood of the new and everlasting covenant. It will be shed for you and for all men that sins may be forgiven." The congregation can know the power of God's gift to make them one as the celebrants invoke the Holy Spirit in Canon Three: "Grant that we who are nourished by his body and blood may be filled with his Holy Spirit and become one body, one spirit in Christ."

The congregation can know unity in that Spirit which unites it in the communion of saints. From that knowledge there arises spontaneously the desire to proclaim and invoke the saints beginning with Mary, the virgin Mother of God, the privileged one, first among all the disciples, true Mother of God and woman of faith. The list of the apostles and saints can flow naturally as do the prayers for the Pope, the local bishop and the entire People of God. The Spirit of God can so enlarge our hearts that we earnestly desire to pray for the whole Church and be a part of the burdens of all.

The Doxology: "through him, with him and in him in the unity of the Holy Spirit all glory and honor is yours Almighty Father for ever and ever" is a time of triumphal glorious proclamation. It should be accompanied with full voice, music and a standing acknowledgment in response.

The Lord's Prayer is a time of intimacy. Through the Holy Spirit we are able to know and proclaim God as our Father. We know the binding force of the Spirit in the Kiss of Peace and the eternal value of the Lamb of God slain for our sins as we prepare to receive. The Communion rite proclaims the healing nature and power in the Body and Blood of the Lord: the celebrant prays that "it bring health in mind and body." The people respond, "only say the word and I shall be healed." The charismatic renewal has emphasized the reality of these words and thousands of American Catholics now expect and receive real healings in Communion. This brings into practice the teaching of the

Church Fathers that the Eucharist is the ordinary sacrament of healing.

The remainder of the Eucharist concentrates on
thanksgiving, again praising in the Spirit of God and
sending one another forth to perform the work of the
Lord. The final song should have special vibrancy and a
special note of victory as the local family of God goes
forth in the victory of the Lord Jesus Christ.

The Eucharist has special and central meaning on the
Sabbath, the Sunday celebration. Our people need to
experience the beauty of the Sabbath. This is the Lord's
day, the day of rest and re-creation. This refreshment is
to come because we are treating the day as belonging to
the Lord. We need to center on him, make praising him,
hearing his word and celebrating his Eucharist the central event. We need to realize that it is the Sabbath
which gives meaning to the other six days. Monday to
Saturday exist for the Sabbath which is the only day to
last forever. We will be celebrating an eternal Sabbath
in heaven. We should be caught up in the life of the Lord
on that day. God's life has no toil, no anxiety, no fear, no
hatred or dissension and our lives can be uplifted by
participating in the God-life we have received. Truly on
the Sabbath we are to live as fully as possible the life of
the Family of God. This message needs to be proclaimed
as part of the normal life of Christians. It comprises the
special basis for the Sunday Eucharist.

While I have developed all sacraments in the light of
community in the book *And Their Eyes Were Opened-
Encountering Jesus in the Sacraments*, let me sketch
here briefly the core of the other four sacraments as
celebrated in the context of a communal life.

Penance: Without a community life, the Sacrament of
Penance makes little sense. It becomes an individual

matter of penitent and priest, of guilt removed by absolution, going out again to strive individually to be good until once again the obstacles, the temptations are too great. With this mentality, this approach it is understandable that people say, "Why can't I just tell God?—he'll forgive me. Why do I have to go to a priest?" But once this sacrament is seen in the light of Christian community, it becomes a gift to be celebrated. When I am bonded together with others in committed relationships, my sin, my weakness, affects the whole body. Where I have harmed others, I eagerly desire to repair it, to seek forgiveness. But I also bring it to the priest who stands for the community to which I belong—he forgives me with the power of Jesus in the name of all my brothers and sisters. The power of this sacrament enables the priest who seeks it with discernment to find the root cause of the sin confessed. Wisdom, prayer, truth and encouragement are to be offered in that sacrament. Healing, new hope and new life are normally to be expected among those who celebrate this sacrament as part of a community.

Confirmation: While Confirmation was seen by the early Church as a Sacrament of Initiation and given with Baptism and Eucharist, nevertheless in light of today's pastoral practice let us examine what this sacrament should celebrate. Let us view this sacrament in the context of the normal Christian life by posing several questions:

Should not the young person be *confirmed* in the gifts he has already had an opportunity to manifest in service within the Christian community?

Since Confirmation not only confers the Spirit but brings forth the power of the Spirit should we not see that Spirit manifested in new power to pray, new

strength to witness to his/her faith, the beginnings of
new spiritual gifts as Paul speaks of in 1 Cor. 12? Those
gifts are given as I have said to build and strengthen not
only the individual but the life of the community. What
happens then when there is no community? Is it not
logical that gifts therefore lie dormant and we miss out
on the portion of our inheritance God wants us to experience?

Should not the newly confirmed be given new responsibilities in prayer, study, and religious service because
they now have new power to discharge these
responsibilities?

What have we done to this sacramental gift of God
when we relegate it to an additional weekly instruction
in doctrine, celebrate the ritual followed by gifts and a
party and then treat the person no differently than before?

Orders: In this sacrament we need to see the priest not
just as one who celebrates Mass, ministers the sacraments and administers the parish. He is Shepherd—he
is called forth to govern, to oversee, to pastor the lives of
people. He is chief intercessor standing between the
people and their God. He is defender, protector, speaker
of God's truth to his people. Such a man should be
called forth by the people with whom he lives and works
and prays. They are the ones to see his gifts, his very life
among them. Study for the priesthood is not to be an
individual matter between a young man and his vocation director but without a living community it is rele-
gated to that kind of personal choice.

A man with a pastoral heart and mind encouraged by
his people, called forth, educated and ordained by his
Bishop, can then discern and call forth the gifts and
ministries of his people. He should coordinate and di-

rect those gifts of the Christian people. Never did God intend that a pastor do it all by himself or simply delegate certain administrative and financial duties to a parish council.

Normal church life—a Church alive—is one where the spiritual gifts and material talents of all God's people are at work to build community under the pastoral oversight of the shepherd.

Anointing of the Sick: In James 5:14 we read:

> Is any among you sick? Let him call for the elders of the Church and let them pray over him, anointing him with oil in the name of the Lord; and the prayer of faith will save the sick man and the Lord will raise him up; and if he has committed sins he will be forgiven.

That is the scriptural basis for the Sacrament of the Sick. It is to be a time when those called forth to govern and pastor God's people come to intercede for their sick brother or sister, confident that in their expectant faith God will either heal that person in this life which should be the normal level of expectation or that he will take that person to himself in peace. But in either case he will raise that person up unto life.

By mentioning the elders, scripture designates more than a single priest and implicitly calls the body of mature believers to join in prayer, for it is the prayer in faith that reclaims the ill person. Doctors and medicine are God's gifts too and should be used but both prayer and medical care should be exercised with the expectant faith that God does want to bless, heal and restore us just as he did when he walked on our earth.

Our vision is so small these days we don't expect God to act, to change us, to intervene according to his will in our lives. But he does! Those who surrender to Jesus as Lord, open up to the power of his Spirit to direct and empower our lives will experience the power of being a new creation in both body and spirit. (2 Cor. 5:17)

From our experience we can say, "Show me your communal life and I will tell you your potential for sacramental celebration. If you show me a scattered, fragmented group of Christians, with little common identity or commitment to one another, I will tell you to be patient and build slowly, yet be prepared to see new life stunted in its growth. If you show me a community of people who know their identity as sons and daughters of the Father and who live out their commitments to one another as brothers and sisters, then I will speak with you about liturgical planning and celebration of the sacraments which can bring joy to your local Church.

Once we recognize these truths, we can begin to be a part of establishing a new set of priorities for the renewal of the parish. Such priorities should include personal conversion of the members of the parish and development of a personal relationship with the Lord. Out of that flows the development of committed relationships among the members of the parish, which finds expression in spiritual and practical care for one another's lives.

Such priorities will enable pastors and parishioners to find their way to the center of God's plan. From that vantage point, God's people will come to know the power and wisdom of his Spirit as they have not known it before.

In this next chapter I want to write about what is going on in the charismatic renewal relative to Ecumenism and the kind of commitment the Church calls us to make to this work of the Spirit.

I have purposely placed this area last in the book because I believe a right understanding of Ecumenism for Catholics can flow only from the understanding of how God's Spirit is calling the people of the Roman Catholic Church to be renewed.

Charismatics a major force

NATIONAL CATHOLIC REPORTER, Aug. 12, 1977, p. 1

Suenens calls gathering ecumenical triumph

By Jason Petosa
NCR National Affairs

THE CATHOLIC WEEKLY (serving the Diocese of Kalamazoo), Friday, July 29, 1977

Messianic Jews Discuss Dichotomy at Conferer

By Susan Forscutt
A Member of the Staff

Faced with the conflict of being and followers of Christ, hun lews pondered

ed, cultural, establishment Son," said one participant.

The fears, frustrations and future of the believers in the New Man were dis cussed by seven religious leaders at the session.

crisis and the ideologies were two

outlined plan worship ser gogue servic throughout

"There is a Jewish fu ture," Sterr Jesus, we theology.

Charismatic Meet: 'Majo Step to Christian Unity'

By RICHARD W. DAW
KANSAS CITY, Mo. (NC)

CATHOLICS concluded their renewal
Thousands of

he said.
ague is professor and Scripture at 's College of the Toronto.
nference drew to Kevin M. Rana man of the con ning committee, ament on behalf

50,000 at Charismatic conference in Kansas City

FRIDAY, JULY 22, 1977

Los Angeles Times, July 22, 1977

The New York Tim

Charismatics Gather for Unique Religious Conclave

BY RUSSELL CHANDLER
Times Religion Writer

New Testament Book of Acts. These lude supernatural healing, visions, and speaking in tongues. on figures here in the partici

Charismatic leader says

s 'not the Chu ope of t Speal wo gr who n ontin he to dr. we'r reede ome and w ork p

'Charismatic Christia Seek to Infuse the Fa With Their Joyous Sp

By KENNETH A. BRIGGS
Special to The New York Times

houts by an infusion of the Hol known among them orn of the H

Ecumenism seen as key to renewal

By DAVID E. ANDERSON
UPI Religion Writer

KANSAS CITY, Mo. — Charismatics gathered in an unprecedented ecu menical meeting, were warned Thursday that when the "charismatic renewal loses its ecu menical character it tends to shrivel up."

The Rev. Larry Chris tenson, of San Pedro, Calif., chairman of the Lutheran

advance His program, which is to make us one, as He and the Father are one."

At the same time, how ever, Christenson de fended the controversial "gifts of the spirit" that characterize the charis matic movement as necessary for church renewal.

The me

Christenson, however, rebutted traditional theologians who say that a spiritual renewal is possible without the charismatic gifts and termed them essential for this time.

"Christ has chosen in our day to lay particula emphasis

upon these gifts as though we had chosen them on our own initiative," he said. "We did not choose these gifts. The Lord Jesus has chosen to come knocking on these doors, and we have responded, his knock

since the early 1960s has often been the subject of bitter controversy, and in the past some charismat ics have been thrown out of their denomination

CHAPTER SIX

ECUMENISM

The Church cannot be fully "in a state of mission" without being "in a state of unity" and it cannot be "in a state of unity" if it is not "in a state of Renewal." Gospel mission, ecumenism, renewal in the Spirit are but facets of one indivisible reality; only the angles of vision differ[1]

It was mid-July, 1977 . . . mid-summer . . . intense heat . . . Kansas City, Missouri. But, fifty thousand people from many Christian backgrounds came together in the football stadium to hear God speak his word in the power of the Spirit. This gathering was known as the Kansas City Conference on Charismatic Renewal in the Christian Churches.

It was an enormous undertaking. For a year and a half a steering committee of fourteen denominations under the leadership of Dr. Kevin Ranaghan had met to strive for unity in the Spirit, to plan the daily denominational sessions and the nightly ecumenical gatherings in the football stadium. This task was complicated by theolog-

[1] Leon Joseph Cardinal Suenens. *Ecumenism and Charismatic Renewal: Theological and Pastoral Orientations*, Malines Documents 2, (Ann Arbor: Servant Books, 1978) p. viii.

ical and explicit doctrinal differences, by centuries of cultural separation and apologetic controversies. But the leaders of the renewal believed God had called us to this highly symbolic and prophetic work, for the great sign and wonder of Christianity is not healing or prophecy or exorcism but rather "that all may become as you, Father, are in me and I in you that the world may know that you sent me." (John 17:21) Only when Christians are one, will the world stand in awe and, finding no other explanation for this unity, proclaim that Jesus is sent from God to reconcile man to God and establish a kingdom of peace and love among mankind.

Thirteen different denominational and non-denominational bodies came together, prayed and sang and confirmed God's preached word as a body. There was unity in the Spirit among the fifty thousand Baptists, Pentecostals, Presbyterians, Lutherans, Catholics, Episcopalians, Mennonites, Methodists, Orthodox, Messianic Jews and Non-Denominational fellowships which came together to proclaim Jesus as Lord, to proclaim their desire to be one and their belief that the Lord, in fulfillment of his word, will make them one. It was historic and overwhelming. They all sounded alike. The Bishop of the largest Holiness Church in the world shared the pulpit with Cardinal Suenens, the Cardinal Archbishop of Malines-Brussels, Belgium. Ruth Carter Stapleton, the President's sister, spoke before Father Francis Mac-Nutt, a Dominican priest. I spoke immediately preceding the final address of the conference by Rev. James Forbes, a black Pentecostal preacher and professor at Union Theological Seminary. It was historic, but more important, it was prophetic. The meaning of the conference was powerfully taught in the three main addresses by Dr. Kevin Ranaghan, Director of the National Communication Office for the Catholic Charismatic Renewal, Rev. Larry Christenson, leader of the Lutheran Charismatic Renewal and Rev. Bob Mumford, leader of Christian Growth Ministries, a segment of the non-denominational Charismatic Renewal. The message was the same in all three teachings: let's get together, love one another, tolerate and support one another and see ourselves as all parts of the great whole, the great work of God, the Church of Jesus Christ. Let's not ignore our differences or be false with any truth, we don't need "sloopy agape" but we need true love, believing in the one Lord, the one faith, the one baptism, the one God and Father of us all. Ultimately, all true evangelism is ecumenical and all true ecumenism leads to Christian unity. Amen. Come Lord Jesus and save your people.

The conference was not superficial in its dealing with the painful and complicated issue of a divided Christianity. The conference did not promote only joy and praise. There was a deep note of pain and for many the first insight into the pain in God's heart occasioned by the divisions among his people. Ralph Martin gave the prophecy which expressed this pain and remained ringing in the hearts and minds of most of us long after the last conference participant had departed Arrowhead Stadium:

> Mourn and weep for the Body of My Son is broken. Mourn and weep for the Body of My Son is broken. Come before me with sackcloth and ashes. Come before me with tears and mourning for the Body of My Son is broken. I would have made you one new man but the Body of My Son is broken. I would have made you a light on a mountaintop, a city glorious and splendorous that all the world would have seen but the Body of My Son is broken. The light is dim. My people are scattered. The Body of My Son is broken. I gave all I had in the Body and Blood

of My Son. It spilled on the earth. The Body of My Son is broken. Turn from the sins of your fathers and walk in the ways of My Son. Return to the plan of your Father. Return to the purpose of your God. The Body of My Son is broken. Mourn and weep for the Body of My Son is broken.

And so, we mourned and wept. Fifty thousand people knelt in that stadium weeping for their own sins and the sins of their respective denominations that had furthered the division among us. We wept for our prejudice, our bigotry, cruel jokes, our preaching against one another. We begged the Lord of heaven and earth to have mercy upon us. Then, with a firm commitment to intercede for the unity of God's people and never to speak against one another again, we rose to sing, "Holy God, We Praise Thy Name." For the twenty two thousand Catholics present, it was a new and glorious experience to hear that deeply traditional hymn sung with such power by all the different denominations. Such a sign of unity gave tremendous hope to us.

Probably the most challenging and exciting dimension of the charismatic renewal is its strong thrust toward Christian Unity. The charismatic renewal has been characterized by commentators as the most promising and, at times, the most foolhardy of ecumenical activity today. At a time when ecumenism for most Christians means a stew of theological dialogue, Church Unity Week assemblies and a new level of friendliness with former apologetic enemies, the charismatic renewal has launched into ecumenical prayer groups, ecumenical communities, ecumenical conferences and in general, widespread activities in which Christians from different denominations treat each other as brothers and sisters. All this, called grass root ecumenism, moves the hearts of thousands to proclaim: it's possible, we can seriously begin now to pursue our heritage as one Body, the Body of Christ. Others, usually the more reserved or reflective types, point out that so many areas of disagreement in doctrine and diversity in practice remain, that it is unrealistic to dwell on what is held in common and to speak so strongly of the unity ahead.

There is truth in both positions. But there also tends to be falsehood or at least, an insufficient understanding of what is happening in charismatic renewal. Certainly it is naive to believe that there are no differences merely because people now pray together and praise together and recognize the same Spirit in each other. Nor is it sufficient to say that people approach the scriptures in the same way or believe in the same spiritual gifts: being baptized in the Spirit, praying in tongues, healing, deliverance, prophecy and words of wisdom and knowledge. It is still true that Christians have been formed in their denominations and they carry within them a heritage of the original protests that caused the separations. There are real differences on the sacraments particularly Eucharist, Reconcilation (Confession) and Orders. There are vastly divergent views on Mary the Mother of Jesus, on the Pope and infallibility, on purgatory and the communion of saints. One of the first controversies to arise in the renewal is infant baptism. Other issues, less doctrinal but no less real, concern the use of alcoholic drink and tobacco, the literal and fundamental as opposed to the modern exegetical approaches to Scripture. Remarriage and rebaptism are occasions for Catholics to pull back from Protestant companions. The Mass, rosary and veneration of Saints create circumstances when many Protestants quickly question the oneness they hold with their Catholic companions.

While all this reality challenges the appearance of unity, there is still ample evidence of true progress toward oneness. Christians of all denominations affirm that the same Spirit is present in brothers and sisters of different denominations in the renewal. They affirm that they have in common one Lord, one faith, one baptism, one God and Father of them all. (Eph. 4:5–6) They affirm that they pray by the one Spirit and share the common belief in the Bible as the inspired Word of God and minister to one another with the same spiritual gifts. It is a deep moving experience to hear a confirmed truth of God spoken through a brother or sister who has strong denominational differences from oneself. It is overwhelming to realize that whether that person is right doctrinally or whether you are right doctrinally in some areas, God has chosen to speak through both of you. God has not withheld his spiritual gifts from Christians who truly seek his Lordship regardless of their Christian denomination. That is very important. Any analysis of the spiritual gifts, the spiritual fervor and the Christian maturity of those in the charismatic renewal would have to conclude that denomination is no barrier to God's blessings in these areas. Baptists, Catholics, Pentecostals, Presbyterians, Orthodox, Methodists, Lutherans, Mennonites, Episcopalians and Non-Denominationalists, all have members who are baptized in the Spirit, pray in tongues, love one another, minister healing and deliverance, prophesy the Word of God, preach under the anointing of the Spirit and grow in holiness and overall Christian maturity. This is overwhelmingly significant. If God so blesses these Christians, how should we treat them? If God does not withhold his gifts and presence from them, should Christians withhold their gifts and presence? The response of the great majority of the charismatic renewal is NO. They respond: let us follow the action of God; let us be for one another as God is for us. Furthermore, and highly significantly, they testify to a new desire in their hearts for unity, a new drawing to be one with those Christians of other denominations. They testify to the overwhelming reality of the Church and the Body of Christ as embracing all Christians. Many would say that their vision has been expanded and their priorities are changed even though they have not forsaken any of the truths of their own denomination.

How does a Roman Catholic approach all of this? On one hand a Catholic is very committed to a unified Church that is One, Holy, Catholic and Apostolic. A Catholic believes there should be unity of authority in the Church, that the Church should have all marks of holiness found in scripture and tradition, that the Church should be universal throughout the world and that the Church should trace itself by succession to the Apostles and continue to live out the apostolic heritage. These Catholic commitments provide an embracing framework and desire for unity but they also present barriers. How can those who do not accept the unity of authority of bishops and pope be included? How can those who do not accept the means of holiness in the Eucharist and all seven sacraments be united in holiness? How can those who do not accept the apostolic succession of the Pope and bishops be united in apostolicity? How can those who identify their denomination with a definitive geographical district or who allow for many denominations be one in Catholicity? These are hard questions and they should not be brushed aside.

Instead, what is needed again is a following of the movement of God. The work of God today has direction and inspiration. Those in Catholic Charismatic Renewal proclaim the need to be renewed with a complete renewal of the mind. (Romans 12:2) We need to seek God's heart and God's mind and follow God's action. We need to trust God to lead us to unity. We cannot manufacture unity or create it as we would an erector set. We need to be children and to live the Gospel together, respecting one another's differences but willing to live and pray together.

This approach is confirmed in the recently released document by Cardinal Suenens who writes:

> To dwell on spiritual ecumenism does not mean to overlook the importance of ecumenical action in other sectors, such as social, economic or the political. But Providence seems to be assigning to the Charismatic Renewal a specific role, full of promise for the future by making it the instrument of brotherly and profound encounters between Christians, united in a "persevering and unanimous prayer"—a prayer whose prototype was that of the Cenacle in Jerusalem on the eve of Pentecost.[2]

Practically, this means taking a new view on how we do relate. An illustration will help. A few years ago I was authorized by my Bishop to join with a Methodist minister in performing a wedding ceremony for a Catholic man and a Methodist woman. The ceremony took place in the Methodist Church. The Methodist Pastor informed me that since it was his church he would have to conduct the essential elements of the ceremony. He then told me that the essentials were the opening

[2] *Ibid.*

prayer and the homily. I, in turn, could care for the remainder of the ceremony. From my perspective and that of the Roman Catholic Church, the essential element was the exchange of vows, and what confirmed the marriage bond. I concluded these elements in accord with the Catholic Ritual. As a result, each of us conducted that part of the service that was most important to us. Since we agreed as to the ultimate meaning of what we were doing and its effect of binding a man and woman together in marriage for as long as both shall live and in this case, of also celebrating the sacrament of matrimony, we were able to be united in our celebration of Church that day.

This illustrates the kind of process that takes place in most movements toward Christian unity. What is essential to one is not the point of emphasis or concern to the other. All of the major Protestant reformation movements were designed to correct real deficiencies in the life of the Catholic Church. The Catholic Church had many preachers and teachers who distorted the doctrine of indulgences, failed to emphasize the power of God's word in preaching, placed too much emphasis on good works in relationship to faith, emphasized the roles of Mary and the saints without keeping at all times a central emphasis on Jesus and allowed a high degree of superstition and mechanical unreflective prayer to develop as common practice. The leaders of the reformation initially sought to bring renewal in these areas but ultimately led a group of believers to form their own denominational church which emphasized the doctrines that the reformers had preached. The Vatican Council taught that the Church of Jesus Christ subsists in the Roman Catholic Church. The Church of Jesus Christ embraces the Roman Catholic Church and all the true reforms. The One True Church in the eyes of Catholic charismatic leaders will be the rightly reformed Catholic Church. From the Catholic point of view, it will be the Catholic Church now perfected in those areas of distortion. From the Protestant point of view it will be the vindication of the main issues of reformation. Preaching, justification by faith, the centrality of God's inspired word in scripture, the need for personal appropriation of grace life, the need for true repentance for sin and not just the sacramental action of absolution— all these will be affirmed as part of the Church. The Catholic will be able to say the essentials have been retained while the Protestants will proclaim that the most important elements are restored.

What is being discovered through charismatic renewal is a new insight of complementarity. We are used to speaking of the complementary roles of men and women. Husband and wives are not to conflict or compete but are called to complement one another, making one completed whole. This is what is meant by the scriptural phrase: to become two in one flesh.

In the renewal we give great attention to the complementarity in the Body of Christ. St. Paul teaches in 1 Cor. 12 that to each is given a manifestation of the one Spirit and each has need of the other.

> The eye cannot say to the hand "I have no need of you," nor again the head to the feet, "I have no need of you." Now you are the body of Christ and individually members of it. (1 Cor. 12:21, 27)

What we are discovering is that there are different gifts from the different denominations which are to be brought to the One Body, the One True Church of Jesus Christ. The reformation movement did develop to a point so that in some Protestant denominations not only was preaching emphasized but it was developed into a more mature ministry. Similarly, the understanding of salvation and born again experiences, as well as being baptized in the Spirit, were developed in Protestant and Pentecostal denominations. These doctrines and ministries, once mature, complement the traditional Catholic teaching. They do not conflict with it. The Roman Catholic Church believes in the importance of preaching and the living of a full life in the Holy Spirit. Catholic tradition also believes in spiritual experiences as gifts from God to encourage us toward Christian maturity and perfection. The Protestant and Pentecostal denominations can provide a fullness to these already-held beliefs.

Admittedly there are doctrinal disagreements that remain specifically unresolved. Secondly, there are substantial accretions to the original points of reformation. As a result there are barriers that have resulted from four hundred year of apologetic war (that is, denominational debate). Finally, there exist many prejudices based on false information and many other kinds of prejudice that will simply fall away when mature people of different denominations have a commitment to seek truth together.

Catholics must joyfully acknowledge and esteem the truly Christian endowments from our common heritage which are to be found among our separated brethren. It is right and salutary to recognize the riches of Christ and virtuous works in the lives of others who are bearing witness to Christ, sometimes even to the shedding of their blood. For God is always wonderful in His works and worthy of admiration.

Not should we forget that whatever is wrought by the grace of the Holy Spirit in the hearts of our separated brethren can contribute to our own edification. Whatever is truly Christian never conflicts with the genuine interests of the faith; indeed it can always result in a more ample realization of the very mystery of Christ and the Church.

Vatican Documents
Decree on Ecumenism, Article 4

This I believe is the regular experience of leaders in Catholic charismatic renewal who are part of ecumenical prayer groups and communities. They are faithfully living as Catholics but continually finding that their Protestant brothers and sisters can share life in many ways with them. Protestants and Catholic leaders are finding that real unity is the work of the Spirit of God poured out in their hearts. They are finding that they have common roots in the Old Testament, the New Testament, the early Christian communities and centuries of church life in which untold saintly men and women lived the Gospel and handed on a heritage of holiness to their descendants.

The key point is that the leaders in charismatic renewal are finding all this out because they are praying together, ministering together, sharing their lives with one another and in some cases living together under a common covenant. Their lives together are experientially resolving some differences. At times, they are finding that supposed barriers do not exist at all. This does not mean that everything is resolved and that all are one. But great progress is made when Christians from different denominational backgrounds can be faithful to their denominational teaching and still share a communal life in many respects.

We can recall here Cardinal Mercier's words which are cherished by Cardinal Suenens:

—we have to encounter one another in order to know one another;

—to know one another in order to love one another;

—to love one another in order to unite.[3]

Finally, the leaders of the Catholic Charismatic Renewal believe that Christian Unity is an important and essential part of what God is doing in the current charismatic renewal. They believe that God does not want them to reproduce in the renewal the same walls of separation that presently exist among denominations. They believe God wants significant, substantial movement toward Christian Unity through the living out of the life of the Spirit shared by them all. They believe that God is blessing the efforts of true ecumenism in daily life. They do not embrace a type of superficial unity which would ignore the differences as not real or as not needing to be dealt with. These leaders of Catholic Charismatic Renewal hear the Lord calling for a new response today toward unity through daily ecumenical life. They are seeking to respond in a responsible manner which will not make them any less Catholic but more Catholic because they are more ecumenical. They trust God and follow him as to how this unity will essentially be fulfilled.

Ecumenism is the work of the Holy Spirit; let us humbly and ardently open ourselves to his breath, surrender to his action and believe in his active presence in us and in each of our brethren.[4]

[3] Cardinal Mercier. Conversations of Malines (1921–1926) as cited by Cardinal Suenens in *Ecumenism and Charismatic Renewal: Theological and Pastoral Orientations*, p. ix.

[4] Suenens, p. 108.

Indeed, the historical origins of charismatic renewal can be traced back to Pentecostalism which began at the turn of the century in a small farmhouse in Topeka, Kansas where a small group of people were baptized in the Spirit. In 1958, the Pentecostal movement came into the mainline churches with Father Dennis Bennett, an Episcopalian priest, who experienced being baptized in the Spirit in Van Nuys, California. Some of the "descendants" from these events were available to affirm and encourage the Duquesne Weekend Catholics when they were baptized in the Holy Spirit in 1967.

Truly, charismatic renewal is ecumenical in origin, continues ecumenical in practice and has as an explicit goal the unity of all Christians.

Leo Josef Cardinal Suenens, as principal concelebrant, elevates the consecrated host at the Sunday liturgy for Catholic Charismatics assembled for the conference in Kansas City, Mo.

One can tell at a glance there was excellent attendance at the Kansas City Conference for Charismatic Renewal in the Christian Churches. Photo taken in July, 1977.

Photos: New Covenant Magazine

Left to right: Bishop James O. Patterson, Presiding Bishop of the Church of God in Christ; Leo Josef Cardinal Suenens, Archbishop of Malines, Brussels, Belgium; and Thomas F. Zimmerman, General Superintendent of the General Council of The Assemblies of God, Springfield, Mo., shared the speakers' platform.

Charles Simpson of the (nondenominational) Gulf Coast Fellowships; Dr. J. Rodman Williams, President of Melodyland School of Theology, Anaheim, Calif.; and Larry Christianson, Pastor of Trinity Lutheran Church, San Pedro, Calif., and Chairman of Lutheran Charismatic Renewal Services, all pray earnestly for unity or reconciliation within the Body of Christ.

Photos: New Covenant Magazine

CONCLUSION

If the Church is pilgrim, en route to the Promised Land, then charismatic renewal is doubly pilgrim for it has no meaning apart from the Church; it exists only because the Church exists. Furthermore, it is not a movement to achieve permanent identity; it is not even a renewal in the control of men. It is totally and wholly dependent on God's gracious action. If the anointings cease, if there are no prophecies, healings, deliverances, words of knowledge and wisdom, in a word, if there is no "outpouring" of the Spirit, the renewal is finished. It stops when God stops. But God cannot stop unless he decides to change the nature of the Church. For the Catholic Church to be fully the continuation of the Apostolic Church there must be a charismatic renewal. The Church must be renewed, vivified, and empowered by the Holy Spirit with those manifestations of the Spirit which are proclaimed in the scripture.

Not everyone need join a charismatic renewal, but everyone is called to be part of a charismatic church. The charismatic dimension of the Church is being restored because God wills it; it is his plan; it will be. My prayer is that those of us called to be servants of the

131

Lord in this work of renewal and restoration may be faithful so that we may have the Church God intends and not make it necessary for him to start over with others. May the Lord bless you and lead you to the place he has for you.

APPENDICES

REPORT OF THE AMERICAN BISHOPS, 1969

The following is the report of the Committee on Doctrine of the National Conference of Catholic Bishops submitted to the bishops in their meeting in Washington, D.C., Nov. 14, 1969. The report was presented by Bishop Alexander Zaleski of Lansing, Michigan, Chairman of the Committee:

Beginning in 1967, the so-called Pentecostal movement has spread among our Catholic faithful. It has attracted especially college students. This report will restrict itself to the phenomenon among Catholics. It does not intend to treat classic Pentecostalism as it appears in certain Protestant ecclesial communities.

In the Catholic Church the reaction to this movement seems to be one of caution and somewhat unhappy. Judgments are often based on superficial knowledge. It seems to be too soon to draw definitive conclusions regarding the phenomenon and more scholarly research is needed. For one reason or another the understanding of this movement is colored by emotionalism. For this there is some historical justification and we live with a suspicion of unusual religious experience. We are also face to face with socially somewhat unacceptable norms of religious behavior. It should be kept in mind that this phenomenon is not a movement in the full sense of the word. It has no national structure and each individual prayer meeting may differ from another.

Many would prefer to speak of it as a charismatic renewal. In calling it a Pentecostal movement we must be careful to disassociate it from classic Pentecostalism as it appears in Protestant denominations, such as the Assemblies of God, the United Pentecostal Church and others. The Pentecostal movement in the Catholic Church is not the acceptance of the ideology or practices of any denomination, but likes to consider itself a renewal in the spirit of the first Pentecost. It would be an error to suppose that the emotional, demonstrative style of prayer characteristic of the Protestant denominations has been adopted by Catholic Pentecostals. The Catholic prayer groups tend to be quiet and somewhat reserved. It is true that in some cases it has attracted emotionally unstable people. Those who come with such a disposition usually do not continue. Participants in these prayer meetings can also exclude them. In this they are not always successful.

It must be admitted that theologically the movement has legitimate reasons for existence. It has a strong biblical basis. It would be difficult to inhibit the work of the Spirit which manifested itself so abundantly in the early Church. The participants in the Catholic Pentecostal movement claim that they receive certain charismatic gifts. Admittedly, there have been abuses, but the cure is not a denial of their existence but their proper use. We still need further research on the matter of charismatic gifts. Certainly, the recent Vatican Council presumes that the Spirit is active continuously in the Church.

Perhaps our most prudent way to judge the validity of the claims of the Pentecostal Movement is to observe the effects on those who participate in the prayer meetings. There are many indications that this participation leads to a better understanding of the role the Christian plays in the Church. Many have experienced progress in their spiritual life. They are attracted to the reading of the scriptures and a deeper understanding of their faith. They seem to grow in their attachment to certain established devotional patterns such as devotion to the real presence and the rosary.

It is the conclusion of the Committee on Doctrine that the movement should at this point not be inhibited but allowed to develop. Certain cautions, however, must be expressed. Proper supervision can be effectively exercised only if the bishops keep in mind their pastoral responsibility to oversee and guide this movement in the Church. We must be on guard that they avoid the mistakes of classic Pentecostalism. It must be recognized that in our culture there is a tendency to substitute religious experience for religious doctrine. In practice we recommend that bishops involve prudent priests to be associated with this movement. Such involvement and guidance would be welcomed by the Catholic Pentecostals.

A STATEMENT OF THE THEOLOGICAL BASIS OF THE CATHOLIC CHARISMATIC RENEWAL

The following statement was drawn up during the International Conference in Rome at the suggestion of Cardinal Suenens. Father Kilian McDonnell was asked to prepare the preliminary draft. A small group of theologians discussed the text with Father McDonnell and aided in its revision. The final draft was presented to conference participants, but was not publicly discussed or voted upon. It should be viewed as a statement of the theological basis of the Catholic Charismatic Renewal, and not as an official pronouncement of the conference. Working with Father McDonnell were Fathers Salvador Carrillo from Mexico, Albert de Monléon, O.P. from France, Francis Martin from Canada, Donatien Mollat from Rome, Heribert Mühlen from Germany, and Francis Sullivan, S.J. from Rome.

The author of this statement intends to describe in brief form the theological basis of the Catholic Charis-

matic Renewal. It is directed to those outside of the
renewal who seek to understand it.

Those involved in the renewal have as their purpose
the proclamation of the Gospel and the promised restoration of all men in Christ which "has already begun in
Christ, is carried forward in the mission of the Holy
Spirit, and through him continues in the Church." (Lumen Gentium, art. 48).

The Catholic Charismatic Renewal has as its basis the
Gospel of Jesus Christ. Without reservation those in the
renewal wish to embrace the full mystery hidden from
all ages in the Father, revealed in the Son, and demonstrated in the Holy Spirit. There is no other Gospel than
that of Jesus Christ, crucified and risen.

Without wishing to absolutize the Acts of the Apostles,
many see the central theological intuition of the renewal
described in Acts. Jesus, crucified and risen, sends the
Spirit. "Being therefore exalted at the right hand of
God, and having received from the Father the Promise of
the Holy Spirit, he has poured out this which you see
and hear." (Acts 2:33) Jesus both receives and sends the
Spirit. The outpouring of the Spirit results in baptism
(Acts 2:38), and the birth of Christian communities (Acts
2:41). These communities are built up by the teaching of
the apostle, fellowship (koinonia), eucharistic celebration and common prayer. "And they devoted themselves
to the apostles' teaching and fellowship, to the breaking
of bread and the prayers." (Acts 2:42) Charisms appear
among the Apostolic community for the upbuilding of
the Church. "Many signs and wonders were done
through the apostles." (Acts 2:43) The experience of the
Spirit's presence and power is directed specifically to
witness and mission, and is related to the Lordship of
Jesus. "You shall receive power when the Holy Spirit
has come upon you; and you shall be my witnesses in

Jerusalem and in all Judea and Samaria and to the ends of the earth." (Acts 1:8)

Those in the renewal do not seek to isolate certain New Testament witness. The Gospel in its New Testament expression did not isolate the Spirit and the coming to visibility of the Spirit in the charisms from the Lordship of Jesus, and the full proclamation of the Kingdom. Both the Spirit and the full spectrum of his charisms are integral to the Gospel of Jesus and were accepted by the New Testament communities as belonging to the meaning of a Christian and to ecclesial life.

Our hearing of the Gospel takes place within a tradition and history which has formed us and of which we are a part. This tradition joins us to the Gospel while this history separates us in time from the Gospel as it was preached and experienced in the early Church.

The Church preaches the same Gospel which was preached by the Apostles. But the renewal asks whether the history out of which we come has the same kind of awareness and the expectations as the early Church had and preached. Many Catholic charismatics point out how contemporary awareness and expectations differ from that of the early Christians. If our awareness of what it means to be "in Christ" and "to walk in the Spirit" differs from that of the early Church, and if we have more limited expectations than they did of how the Spirit comes to visibility in the charisms for the service of the Church and the world, then would this not have a profound effect upon worship, evangelization, and engagement in the life of the world? Those within the charismatic renewal make no claim to a special spiritual endowment or to a special grace which distinguishes those involved in the renewal from others not so involved. If they differ at all, they differ in awareness and expectations and therefore in experience. The purpose of the renewal is not to bring to the Church something she does not have, but to bring to the local churches and the Church universal to Jesus Christ, and to widen the expectations of how the Spirit comes to visibility in the charisms within the life of the Church.

Persons within the renewal wish to point to aspects of the Gospel without attributing an undue importance to them. In particular, they wish to call attention to the manner in which the Holy Spirit and the charisms are related to the Lordship of Jesus, the glory of the Father, the service of the Church and world.

If Catholic charismatics were asked in more specific terms to describe the theological basis of the renewal, they would have to say that theological research and reflection have not been sufficient to permit a final answer. There is a further difficulty which those in the renewal, as those not involved, have in assessing the work of the Spirit. The very nature of the Holy Spirit, who is Breath, involves a difficulty of a different kind from that present when speaking of Jesus, who is Word. However, an attempt will be made to give some explanation of the theological foundations of the renewal. Without prejudice to other explanations the author gives a theological-sacramental formulation which represents the most widely accepted view within the renewal.

To one who reads the literature coming out of the renewal, it becomes obvious that those who write from within the renewal wish to be Catholic and wish to situate the renewal within the Catholic theological tradition. This is an expression, one of many, of the fidelity of the renewal to the Church.

The Spirit and the charisms through which the Spirit comes to visibility belong to the nature of the Church, which is the Body of Christ. The Spirit and his charisms are constitutive of the Church and are not added to an already existing body of Christ. Without the Spirit and his charisms there is no Church. Therefore there is no group or no movement within the Church which can claim the Spirit and his charisms in any exclusive way. If the Spirit and his charisms belong to the nature of the Church they also belong to the nature of the Christian life in its communitarian and individual expression.

St. Paul defines the Christian in terms of both Christ and the Spirit. "Anyone who does not have the Spirit of Christ does not belong to him." (Rom. 8:9) In the Gospels, that which distinguishes the messianic role of Jesus from the role of John the Baptist is that Jesus baptizes in the Holy Spirit. In particular, by the sacrament of baptism one becomes a member of the Body of Christ because in baptism one receives the Spirit. "For by one Spirit we were all baptized into one body—Jews or Greeks, slaves or free—all were made to drink of the one Spirit." (1 Cor. 12–13) The New Testament describes in various ways the process by which one becomes a Christian: it is a process under the aegis of faith. The anointing of faith (1 John 2:20, 27) precedes and accompanies conversion, which is a "turning to God from idols to serve the living and true God and to await his Son from heaven, whom he raised from the dead." (1 Thess. 1:9–10) Conversion leads to baptism, the forgiveness of sins, and the receiving of the Holy Spirit, this faith process is admirably summed up in the conclusion of St. Peter's speech at Pentecost itself: "When they heard these things, they were cut to the heart (faith—cf Acts 15:9) and said to Peter and the other apostles. 'What shall we do, brothers?' and Peter said to them: 'Be converted, and let each one of you be baptized in the name of Jesus Christ for the remission of your sins, and you will receive the gift of the Holy Spirit.' " (Acts 2:37–38)

Around these steps of initiation, and the subsequent "walking in the Spirit" (Gal. 5:16), we can group many of the other New Testament expressions that refer to the process of becoming a Christian: baptism (Rom. 6), illumination (Heb. 6:4), baptized in the Holy Spirit (Acts 1:5), to become a new creature (Gal. 6:15), to be filled with the Holy Spirit (Acts 2:4), to receive the Spirit (Gal 3:2), receiving the gifts and call of God (Rom. 11:29), entrance into the new covenant (Heb. 8:6; 12:24), new birth (1 Pet. 1:23; John 3:3), being born of water and the Spirit (John 3:5).

The decisive Christian-constituting coming of the Spirit is related to the celebration of the Christian initiation (baptism, confirmation, Eucharist). Christian initiation is the effective sign of the Spirit's bestowal. The early Christian communities not only received the Spirit during the celebration of initiation, but expected that the Spirit would demonstrate his power by the transformation he would effect in their lives. To receive the Spirit was to change. Further, they expected that the Spirit would come to visibility along the full spectrum of his charisms in the community, which included, but by no means were limited to, such charisms as helping, administration, prophecy, and tongues (1 Cor. 12:28; cf. Rom. 12:6–8).

The charisms of the Spirit are without number and they constitute the means by which each member of the Church ministers to the whole body. Charisms are essentially ministerial functions directed outward for the building up of the body and the service of the world rather than exclusively inward toward the edification of the individual. The Spirit comes to visibility in a service ministerial function in each Christian. No Christian is without a ministry in and for the Church and world.

One of the things which distinguishes the local and universal Church today from a community in the early Church is that the contemporary Church is not aware of some of the charisms of the Spirit as real possibilities for its life. The contemporary Church has more limited expectations as to how the Spirit comes to visibility. One of the reasons for the restricted expectations is the tendency to describe the assistance of the Holy Spirit primarily in terms of the hierarchical ministry.

Persons in the renewal make no distinction between the essential content of initiation celebrated in the communities of the early Church and that celebrated in the Church today. In both the Spirit is and was received. Today, however, Christians generally have a more limited expectation, awareness and openness as to how the Spirit comes to visibility in the life of the community. If the expectation is limited, so will be the experience of the Spirit in the Church's life. The modality of the Church's life in the Spirit is affected by the Church's expectations. People within the renewal wish to widen the expectations of the local churches and the Church universal so that the full spectrum of the charisms become real possibilities for the total life of the Church. In no way do those involved in the renewal wish to restrict the Church's theological and pastoral attention to the more prophetic charisms. Those in the renewal recognize that an excessive attention to the charisms of the Spirit results in a basic distortion of the Gospel. The charisms are not ends in themselves. But they contribute to that fullness of life in Christ and the Holy Spirit to which the Church is called.

The charismatic renewal, therefore, has its theological foundations in the celebration of initiation and calls for a renewal of baptismal consciousness broadly conceived, that is, "That we might understand the gifts bestowed on us." (1 Cor. 2:12) Those in the renewal urge that the Church open itself to that life received in Christian initiation so that it may attain its fullest expression.

The charismatic renewal is based on the assumption that the Holy Spirit is sovereign and free. He blows when, where, and how he wills. Though the Spirit takes persons and local churches where they are, the Spirit in no radical way is dependent on the subjective dispositions of persons or communities. The Holy Spirit has and retains the initiative at every moment of the community's life.

Some attention should be paid to aspects of the renewal which raise questions in the minds of those who are not participants. Reference was made to the more limited expectations of many in the contemporary Church in comparison to the wider expectations of the early Church. The kind of repristination which renewals represent turns their attention with a kind of inevitability to the life of the New Testament churches. However commendable this return to the New Testament witness is, it should not be forgotten that in the course of the Church's history the Holy Spirit and his charisms were not absent. The Holy Spirit manifested himself in a multiplicity of ways in various epochs of the Church. One could mention the lay monastic movements, the founding of religious orders, the prayer gifts in the Church's mystical tradition, the social awareness as manifested in the papal encyclicals, the movements of political and social engagement. Though the modality in which the Spirit is manifesting himself today appears to take a new form, one cannot suggest that the charismatic manifestations began with what is called the Catholic Charismatic Renewal.

Many of the charisms present no problems to persons not involved in the charismatic renewal. However, the charism of tongues does present a problem. It is also clear that the Catholic renewal is not characterized by an insistence that praying in tongues is in any necessary way tied to the spiritual realities received in initiation. Many outside of the renewal attribute a centrality to tongues which is not reflected in most sectors of the renewal. On the other hand persons involved in the renewal rightly point out that this charism was quite common in the New Testament communities. Those who stand outside the renewal attempting to evaluate the charism of tongues will fail if it is not understood in the framework of prayer. It is essentially a prayer gift enabling many using it to pray at a deeper level. If those within the movement esteem this charism, it is because they want to pray better and the charism of tongues helps them to do that. For a sizeable number of persons who pray in tongues, this is only one of a number of forms of prayer. They also engaged in liturgical prayer, eucharistic celebrations, and in other forms of public and private devotion. This charism, whose existence in the New Testament communities and in early post-apostolic times is well attested, should neither be given undue attention nor despised. Since it is the lowest of the charisms, it should not be a matter of surprise that it is so common.

Another feature of the renewal which causes confusion is the use of the phrase "baptism in the Holy Spirit." For historical reasons, many Catholics in the renewal have adopted this phrase, already current among classical Pentecostals, to describe the experience through which they came into a new awareness of the presence and power of the Spirit in their lives.

But there is a problem in the use of the phrase, as it

could be taken to mean that only those who have had a particular kind of experience of the Spirit have really been baptized in the Spirit. This is not the case, since every valid and fruitful Christian initiation confers "the gift of the Holy Spirit" (Acts 2:38), and "to be baptized in the Holy Spirit" is simply another scriptural way of saying "to receive the Holy Spirit."

Hence, many prefer to use other expressions to describe what is happening in the charismatic renewal. Among the alternatives which have been proposed are: "release of the Spirit," "renewal of the sacraments of initiation," "a release of the power to witness to the faith," "actualization of gifts already received in potency," "manifestation of baptism whereby the hidden grace given in baptism breaks through into conscious experience," "reviviscence of the sacraments of initiation." These are all ways of saying that the power of the Holy Spirit, given in Christian initiation, but hitherto unexperienced, becomes a matter of personal conscious experience.

The emergence of the graces of Christian initiation into conscious experience can happen without any emotional elevation. Experience should not be equated with feelings even though feelings of joy, peace, and love may be present. Furthermore, experience can occur in a growth pattern. That is to say that the emergence of the graces of initiation into conscious experience can be a gradual process, without any peak experiences or without what are called "mountaintop experiences." There is no given moment which one could name as that moment in which the emergence into consciousness took place. There is only the gradual growth extending over months and even years.

Besides this growth pattern of experience, there is what might be called a crisis pattern. This occurs when one can date with some precision the moment when the graces of initiation emerged into conscious experience. The crisis pattern is less familiar to Catholic theological cultures, but is in fact the manner in which many Catholics within the renewal (and outside it) experience the emergence of baptismal grace into consciousness. Both the growth pattern and the crisis pattern should be looked upon as authentic ways of realizing the graces of initiation at the conscious level.

There are many objective elements in the renewal as in the whole Catholic tradition: the celebration of initiation, obedience to the teaching magisterium of the Church and to its discipline, eucharistic celebration, the sacrament of penance, and the sacred Scriptures. One of the more subjective elements is this affirmation of the commitment made at initiation. The persons involved in the renewal emphasize the necessity of personal commitment. As an adult, one cannot be a Christian by proxy. One can only be a Christian by personal commitment. Each adult must say yes to the baptism received as an infant. This move toward personal decision and personal commitment is in keeping with the more personal and explicit adherence to faith taught by *Gaudium et Spes, art. 7.* The constitution speaks of a "a more critical ability to distinguish religion from a magical view of the world and from the superstitions which still circulate." This more critical ability "purifies religion and exacts day by day a more personal and explicit adherence to faith. As a result, many persons are achieving a more vivid sense of God."

If one were to point to the strengths of the renewal, one would mention the genuine conversion experience which leads to a living faith, a profound love of prayer, a love of the Eucharist, a new appreciation for the sacrament of penance, healing of interpersonal relationships, moral transformation, renewed sense of discipleship, awareness of the necessity of firm doctrinal basis, fidelity to the bishops and to the Pope. In some places, especially in Mexico and South America, involvement in the charismatic renewal has meant a new level of engagement in social and political programs. Pervading all these areas is the sense of the presence of the person of Christ, the power of the Spirit, and the glory of the Father. The response to presence is most characteristically praise.

The strengths of the renewal may be instruments for the transformation of the interior life of the Church. Many people, in fact, need a new assurance of faith and a renewed life of prayer. It is well known that many have ceased to pray. This is true even of priests.

The strengths of the renewal can lead to social and political action based not on class hatred, but love of the oppressors and prayer for them. Prayer for the oppressors in no way lessens the struggle against them and against the structures of poverty and violence. It only means a more radically Christian style of social and political action.

There are also problem areas. There is some uncritical acceptance of prophecy and tongues without sufficient discernment as to what comes from the Holy Spirit and what comes from the human psyche. Discernment of spirits is one of the major ongoing problems of the renewal. It should be remembered that the final judgment as to the authenticity of charisms "belongs to those who preside over the Church and to whose special competence it belongs not to extinguish the Spirit, but to test all things and hold fast to that which is good" (Lumen Gentium, art. 12).

There is also present in some quarters an exaggerated

supernaturalism with regard to the charisms, together with an undue preoccupation with them. Sometimes one meets persons in the renewal who attribute too quickly to demonic influence a manifestation which is judged not to be of God. Occasionally views are expressed which would indicate that when one has the Gospel one does not need the Church. At the sacramental level there are some who oppose the subjective experience of salvation to the celebration of the sacraments. Insufficient attention is sometimes paid to the theological training of persons whom the various communities judge to be called to specific ministries. Some place in false opposition the necessity of the transforming power of the Spirit and the necessity of theological training. There is reluctance among some leaders to listen carefully to criticism which emerges both from within the renewal and outside it. Finally, some within the renewal have not drawn the inevitable social implications of life in Christ and the Spirit. In some cases there is real social engagement, but the involvement is superficial in that it does not touch the structures of oppression and injustice.

An attempt has been made to formulate the most widely accepted view of the theological-sacramental basis of the renewal, that is, in relation to the celebration of initiation. Something has been said about the strengths of the renewal and about the specific problem areas. A final word should be said about the relation of the Catholic Charismatic Renewal to other renewals. Those involved in the Catholic Renewal recognize that there are other renewals within other ecclesial communities and churches, as well as outside of them, which give quite different theological explanations for the same spiritual realities. Even though the theological formulations vary, and even though the understanding of Christian revelation differs in important ways, those within the renewal recognize the presence of the Spirit in those who proclaim the Lordship of Jesus to the glory of the Father. That presence in all streams of the renewal is the bond of their unity.

POPE PAUL ADDRESSES THE CHARISMATIC RENEWAL

On Monday, May 19, 1975, the last day of the International Charismatic Conference, Pope Paul VI personally addressed the more than ten thousand conference participants to an audience in St. Peter's Basilica. The following is an official translation of his prepared text which was distributed by the Vatican Press office on May 19. The Pope gave his main address in French, followed by a summary in Spanish and English. He then spoke informally to the conference in Italian.

You have chosen the city of Rome in this Holy Year to celebrate your Third International Congress, dear sons and daughters; you have asked us to meet you today and to address you: you have wished thereby to show your attachment to the church founded by Jesus Christ and to everything that this See of Peter represents for you. This strong desire to situate yourselves in the church is an authentic sign of the action of the Holy Spirit. For God became man in Jesus Christ, of whom the church is the mystical body; and it is in the church that the Spirit of Christ was communicated on the day of Pentecost when he came down upon the apostles gathered in the "upper room," "in continuous prayer," with Mary, the mother of Jesus (see Acts 1:13–14).

As we said last October in the presence of some of you, the church and the world need more than ever that "the miracle of Pentecost should continue in history" (L'Osservatore Romano, October 17, 1974). In fact, inebriated by his conquests, modern man has finished by imagining, according to the expression used by the last council, that he is free "to be an end unto himself, the sole artisan and creator of his own history" (Gaudium et Spes [Pastoral Constitution on the Church in the Modern World], 20). Alas! Among how many of those very people who continue by tradition to profess God's existence and through duty to render him worship God has become a stranger in their lives!

Nothing is more necessary to this more and more secularized world than the witness of this "spiritual renewal" that we see the Holy Spirit evoking in the most diverse regions and milieux. The manifestations of this renewal are varied: a profound communion of souls, intimate contact with God, in fidelity to the commitments undertaken at Baptism, in prayer—frequently in group prayer—in which each person, expressing himself freely, aids, sustains, and fosters the prayer of the others and, at the basis of everything, a personal conviction, which does not have its source solely in a teaching received by faith, but also in a certain lived experience. This lived experience shows that without God man can do nothing, that with him, on the other hand, everything becomes possible: hence this need to praise God, thank him, celebrate the marvels that he works everywhere about us and with us. Human existence rediscovers its "relationship to God," what is called the "vertical dimension," without which man is irremediably crippled. Not of course that this "search for God" appears as a desire for conquest or possession; it wished to be a pure acceptance of him who loves us and gives himself freely to us, desiring, because he loves us, to communicate to us a life that we have to receive freely from him, but not without a humble fidelity on our part. And this fidelity must know how to unite action to faith according to the teaching of St. James: "For as the body apart from the spirit is dead, so faith apart from works is dead" (James 2:26).

How then could this "spiritual renewal" not be a "chance" for the Church and for the world? And how, in this case, could one not take all the means to ensure that it remains so?

These means, dear sons and daughters, the Holy Spirit will certainly wish to show you himself, according to the wisdom of those whom the Holy Spirit himself has established as "guardians, to feed the church of God" (Acts 20:28). For it is the Holy Spirit who inspired St. Paul with certain very precise directives, directives that we shall content ourself with recalling to you. To be faithful to them will be for you the best guarantee for the future.

You know the great importance that the Apostle attributed to the "spiritual gifts." "Never try to suppress the Spirit," he wrote to the Thessalonians (1 Thess. 5:19), while immediately adding: "Test everything, hold fast what is good" (v. 21). Thus he considered that a discernment was always necessary, and he entrusted the task of testing to those whom he had placed over the community (see v. 12). With the Corinthians, a few years later, he enters into great detail: in particular, he indicates to them three principles in the light of which they will more easily be able to practice this indispensable discernment.

1. The first principle by which he begins his exposé is fidelity to the authentic doctrine of the faith (1 Cor. 12:1–3). Anything that contradicted it would not come from the Spirit: he who distributes his gifts is the same one who inspired the Scriptures and who assists the living Magisterium of the Church to whom, according to the Catholic faith, Christ entrusted the authentic interpretation of these Scriptures. This is why you experience the need for an ever deeper doctrinal formation: biblical, spiritual, theological. Only a formation such as this, whose authenticity must be guaranteed by the hierarchy, will preserve you from ever-possible deviations and give you the certitude and joy of having served the cause of the gospel without "beating the air" (1 Cor. 9:26).

2. The second principle: all spiritual gifts are to be received with gratitude: and you know that the list is long (1 Cor. 12:4–10; 28–30), and does not claim to be complete (see Rom. 12:6–8; Eph. 6:11). Given, nevertheless, "for the common good" (1 Cor. 12:7), they do not all procure this common good to the same degree. Thus the Corinthians are to "desire the higher gifts" (v. 31), those most useful for the community (see 14:1–5).

The third principle is the most important one in the thought of the Apostle. This principle has suggested to him one of the most beautiful pages, without a doubt, in all literature, to which a recent translator has given an evocative title: "Above all hovers love" (E. Osty). No matter how desirable spiritual goods are—and they are desirable—only the love of charity, agape, makes the Christian perfect; it alone makes people pleasing to God. This love not only presupposes a gift of the Spirit; it implies the active presence of his Person in the heart of the Christian. The Fathers of the Church commented on these verses, vying with one another to explain them. In the words of Saint Fulgentius, to quote just one example: "The Holy Spirit can give every kind of gift without being present himself; on the other hand he proves that he is present by grace when he gives love" (Contra Fabianum, Fragment 28: PL 65, 791). Present in the soul, he communicates to it, with grace, the Most Blessed Trinity's own life, the very love with which the Father loves the Son in the Holy Spirit (John 17:26), the love by which Christ has loved us and by which we, in our turn, can and must love our brethren, that is "not only in word or speech but in deed and in truth" (1 John 3:18).

The tree is judged by its fruits, and St. Paul tells us that "the fruit of the Spirit is love" (Gal. 5:22)—love such as he has just described in his hymn to love. It is to love that are ordered all the gifts which the Spirit distributes to whom he wills, for it is love which builds up (see 1 Cor. 8:1), just as it is love which, after Pentecost, made the first Christians into a community dedicated to fellowship (See Acts 2:42), everyone being "of one heart and soul" (Acts 4:32).

Be faithful to the directives of the great Apostle. And, in accordance with the teaching of the same Apostle, also be faithful to the frequent and worthy celebration of the Eucharist (See 1 Cor. 11:26–29). This is the way that the Lord has chosen in order that we may have his life in us (See John 6:53). In the same way, approach with confidence the Sacrament of Reconciliation. These sacraments express that grace comes to us from God, through the necessary mediation of the church.

Beloved sons and daughters, with the help of the Lord, strong in the intercession of Mary, Mother of the Church, and in communion of faith, charity, and of the apostolate with your Pastors, you will be sure of not deceiving yourselves. And thus you will contribute, for your part, to the renewal of the Church.

Jesus is the Lord! Alleluia!

(The following is the English summary.)

We are happy to greet you, dear sons and daughters, in the affection of Christ Jesus, and in his name to offer you a word of encouragement and exhortation for your Christian lives.

You have gathered here in Rome under the sign of the Holy Year; you are striving in union with the whole Church for renewal - spiritual renewal, authentic renewal, Catholic renewal, renewal in the Holy Spirit. We are pleased to see signs of this renewal: a taste for prayer, contemplation, praising God, attentiveness to the grace of the Holy Spirit, and more assiduous reading of the Sacred Scriptures. We know likewise that you wish to open your hearts to reconciliation with God and your fellow-men.

For all of us this renewal and reconciliation is a further development of the grace of divine adoption, the grace of our sacramental Baptism "into Christ Jesus" and "into his death" (Rom. 6:3), in order that we "might walk in newness of life" (v. 4).

Always give great importance to this Sacrament of Baptism and to the demands that it imposes. St. Paul is quite clear: "You must consider yourselves dead to sin but alive to God in Christ Jesus" (v. 11). This is the immense challenge of genuine sacramental Christian living, in which we must be nourished by the Body and Blood of Christ, renewed by the Sacrament of Penance, sustained by the grace of Confirmation and refreshed by humble and persevering prayer. This is likewise the challenge of opening your hearts to your brethren in need. There are no limits to the challenge of love: the poor and needy and afflicted and suffering across the world and near at hand all cry out to you, as brothers and sisters of Christ, asking for the proof of your love, asking for the word of God, asking for bread, asking for life. They ask to see a reflection of Christ's own sacrificial, self-giving love—love for his Father and love for his brethren.

Yes, dear sons and daughters, this is the will of Jesus: that the world should see your good words, the goodness of your acts, the proof of your Christian lives, and glorify the Father who is in heaven (See Matt. 5:16). This indeed is spiritual renewal and only through the Holy Spirit can it be accomplished. And this is why we do not cease to exhort you earnestly to "desire the higher gifts" (1 Cor. 12:31). This was our thought yesterday, when on the Solemnity of Pentecost we said: "Yes, this is a day of joy, but also a day of resolve and determination: to open ourselves to the Holy Spirit, to remove what is opposed to his action, and to proclaim, in the Christian authenticity of our daily lives, that Jesus is Lord."

(At this point the Pope's official text ends and his informal address in Italian begins.)

Very dear ones: It is permissible to add a few words in Italian (applause), in fact, two messages. One is for those pilgrims who are present by chance at this great assembly.

Firstly, for you: reflect on the two names by which you are designated, "Spiritual Renewal." Where the Spirit is concerned we are immediately alert, immediately happy to welcome the coming of the Holy Spirit. More than that, we invite him, we pray to him, we desire nothing more than that Christians, believing people, should experience an awareness, a worship, a greater joy through the Spirit of God among us. Have we forgotten the Holy Spirit? Certainly not! We want him, we honor him, and we love him, and we invoke him. And you, with your devotion and fervor, you wish to live in the Spirit. (applause) This, (applause) and this should be where your second name comes in—a renewal. It ought to rejuvenate the world, give it back a spirituality, a soul, and religious thought; it ought to reopen its closed lips to prayer and open its mouth to song, to joy, to hymns, and to witnessing. It will be very fortunate for our times, for our brothers, that there should be a generation, your generation of young people, who shout out to the world the glory and the greatness of the God of Pentecost. (Applause) In the hymn which we read this morning in the breviary, and which dates back as far as St. Ambrose in the third or fourth century, there is this phrase which is hard to translate and should be very simple: Laeti, that means "joyfully," bibamus, "we absorb," sobriam, that means "well-defined and well-moderated," profusionem spiritus ("the outpouring of the Spirit"). Laeti bibamus sobriam profusionem spiritus. It could be a formula impressed over your movement: a plan and an approval of the movement.

The second message is for those pilgrims present at this great assembly who do not belong to your movement. They should unite themselves with you to celebrate the feast of Pentecost—the spiritual renewal of the world, of our society, and of our souls—so that they too, devout pilgrims to this center of the Catholic faith, might nourish themselves on the enthusiasm and the spiritual energy with which we must live our religion. And we will say only this: today, either one lives one's faith with devotion, depth, energy, and joy or that faith will die out.

STATISTICAL SYNOPSIS OF THE CATHOLIC CHARISMATIC RENEWAL

The Gallup Poll in the Fall of 1977 estimated that ten percent of the Catholics in the United States are involved in the charismatic renewal. This means that three and a half million Catholics have had some direct contact or involvement in the movement.

The International Directory of Catholic Charismatic Prayer Groups provides data on 3,227 prayer groups in the United States with a formal membership estimated at 175,000.

Eighty percent of those involved in the Catholic Charismatic Renewal are located in the United States.

161

FOR READING AND REFERENCE

Abbott, Walter M. (ed.). *The Documents of Vatican II* New York: Guild Press, 1966.

Bennett, Dennis and Rita. *The Holy Spirit and You.* Plainfield: Logos International, 1971. (Revised edition 1977)

Cavnar, Jim. *Participating in Prayer Meetings.* Ann Arbor: Word of Life, 1974.

Clark, Steve. *Baptized in the Spirit and Spiritual Gifts.* Pecos: Dove Publications, Ann Arbor: Word of Life, 1974.

————. *Confirmation and the Baptism of the Holy Spirit.* Pecos: Dove Publications, 1969.

————. *Growing in Faith.* Notre Dame: Charismatic Renewal Services, 1972.

————. *Building Christian Communities, Strategy for Renewing the Church.* Notre Dame: Ave Maria Press, 1972.

————. *Unordained Elders and Renewal Communities.* New York: Paulist Press, 1976.

Ensley, Eddie. *Sounds of Wonder.* New York: Paulist Press, 1977.

Ghezzi, Bert. *Build with the Lord.* Ann Arbor: Word of Life, 1976.

Harper, Michael. *As at the Beginning, the Twentieth Century Revival.* Plainfield: Logos International, 1965.

──────. *A New Way of Living.* London: Hodder and Stoughton, 1974.

──────. *Power for the Body of Christ.* Plainfield: Logos Books, 1964.

Hinnebusch, Paul. *Praise: A Way of Life.* Notre Dame: Ave Maria Press, 1975.

Laurentin, Rene. *Catholic Pentecostalism.* Garden City: Doubleday, 1977.

MacNutt, Francis O.P., *Healing.* Notre Dame: Ave Maria Press, 1974.

MacNutt, Francis, O.P., *Power to Heal.* Notre Dame: Ave Maria Press, 1977.

Manuel, David. *Like a Mighty River.* Orleans: Rock Harbor Press, 1977.

Martin, George. *Parish Renewal, A Charismatic Approach.* Ann Arbor: Word of Life, 1976.

──────. *Reading Scripture as the Word of God.* Ann Arbor: Word of Life, 1975.

──────. *Healing.* Ann Arbor: Servant Books, 1977.

Martin, Ralph. *Unless the Lord Build the House.* Notre Dame: Ave Maria Press, 1971.

──────. *Hungry for God.* Ann Arbor: Word of Life, 1974.

──────. *Fire on the Earth.* Ann Arbor: Word of Life, 1975.

──────. (comp.). *New Wine, New Skins.* New York: Paulist Press, 1976.

──────. (comp.). *The Spirit and the Church.* New York: Paulist Press, 1976.

──────. (comp.). *Sent by the Spirit.* New York: Paulist Press, 1976.

──────. *Husbands, Wives, Parents, Children.* Ann Arbor: Servant Books, 1978.

McDonnell, Kilian, O.S.B. (ed.). *The Holy Spirit and*

Power, The Catholic Charismatic Renewal. Garden City: Doubleday and Company, Inc., 1975.

———. *Charismatic Renewal and the Churches.* New York: Seabury Press, 1976.

Montague, George. *Riding the Wind*--Learning the Ways of the Spirit. Ann Arbor: Word of Life, 1974.

O'Connor, Edward, C.S.C. (ed.). *The Pentecostal Movement in the Catholic Church.* Notre Dame: Ave Maria Press, 1971.

———. *Perspectives on Charismatic Renewal.* Notre Dame: University of Notre Dame Press, 1975.

Ranaghan, Kevin and Dorothy. *Catholic Pentecostals.* New York: Paulist Press, 1969.

———. *As the Spirit Leads Us.* New York: Paulist Press, 1969.

Ranaghan, Kevin. *The Lord, the Spirit and the Church.* Ann Arbor: Word of Life, 1973.

Randall, John. *In God's Providence*--the Birth of a Catholic Charismatic Parish. Plainfield: Logos International, 1973.

Scanlan, Michael, T.O.R. *The Power in Penance.* Notre Dame: Ave Maria Press, 1972.

———. *Inner Healing.* New York: Paulist Press, 1974.

Scanlan, Michael, T.O.R. and Sister Ann Therese Shields, R.S.M. *And Their Eyes Were Opened, Encountering Jesus in the Sacraments.* Ann Arbor: Servant Books, 1976.

Scanlan, Michael, T.O.R. *Prayers and Blessings from the ROMAN RITUAL With Commentary.* College of Steubenville, (Ohio), 1978.

Sherrill, John. *They Speak with Other Tongues.* New York: Pyramid Books, 1964.

Suenens, Leon Joseph Cardinal. *A New Pentecost?* New York. Seabury Press, 1974.

_____. *Theological and Pastoral Orientations on the Catholic Charismatic Renewal.* Malines Document 1, Ann Arbor: Word of Life, 1974.

_____. *Ecumenism and Charismatic Renewal: Theological and Pastoral Orientations.* Malines Document 2, Ann Arbor: Servant Books, 1978.

Synan, Vinson. *Charismatic Bridges.* Ann Arbor: Word of Life, 1974.

Thomas Aquinas. *Summa Theologica,* Volume 1. New York: Benziger Brothers, Inc., 1947.

Walsh, Rev. Vincent. *A Key to Charismatic Renewal in the Catholic Church.* St. Meinrad: Abbey Press, 1976.

Yocum, Bruce. *Prophecy.* Ann Arbor: Word of Life, 1976.